National Safety Council

Stress
Management

National Safety Council

Stress Management

Editorial, Sales, and Customer Service Offices

Jones and Bartlett Publishers
One Exeter Plaza
Boston, MA 02116
1-800-832-0034
617-859-3900

Jones and Bartlett Publishers International
7 Melrose Terrace
London W6 7RL
England

ISBN 0-86720-980-1

Vice President and Publisher: Clayton E. Jones
Editorial Assistant: Deborah L. Haffner
Production Editor: Mary Cervantes
Manufacturing Buyer: Dana L. Cerrito
Editorial Production Service: Books By Design, Inc.
Cover Design: Hannus Design Associates
Printing and Binding: Banta Company
Cover Printing: John P. Pow Company

Photo credits: pp. ii and 9 David Pratt/Positive Images; p. 1 Larry Williams/Masterfile; p. 2 Robert Rathe/Stock, Boston (l), Charles Gupton/Stock, Boston (r); p. 10 Bruce Ayres/Tony Stone Images; p. 20 Jerry Howard/Positive Images; p. 21 Martin Benjamin/The Image Works (l), North Wind (r); p. 24 Bruce Ayres/Tony Stone Images; p. 25 Rhoda Sidney/The Image Works; p. 26 Jerry Howard/Positive Images; p. 27 David Pratt/Positive Images; p. 32 Bob Daemmrich/Stock, Boston; p. 46 Lori Adamski Peek/Tony Stone Images (l and r); p. 48 Bruce Ayres/Tony Stone Images; p. 49 Lori Adamski Peek/Tony Stone Worldwide (l), Anthony Blake/Tony Stone Worldwide (r); p. 50 Cathlyn Melloan/Tony Stone Images; p. 52 Myrin Borysenko/Mind Body Health Sciences (l), T. Shumsky/The Image Works (r); p. 53 Bonnie Smetts/Pomegranate Publications (l); p. 58 Lori Adamski Peek/Tony Stone Images; p. 64 Jerry Howard/Positive Images; p. 65 Peter Southwick/Stock, Boston; pp. 11, 51, 53(r), 54, 60 Brian Luke Seaward. *Cover:* Jerry Howard/Positive Images; David Pratt/Positive Images; Peter Southwick/Stock, Boston; Larry Williams/Masterfile; Bruce Ayres/Tony Stone Images; Lori Adamski Peek/Tony Stone Worldwide; Brian Luke Seaward.

Printed in the United States of America
98 97 96 95 94   10 9 8 7 6 5 4 3 2 1

Welcome Message

On behalf of the National Safety Council, I welcome you as a participant in our Stress Management Training Program. Our society now recognizes stress as an underlying cause of workplace injuries and illnesses, making it a major safety and health issue. Therefore the relationship between stress and safety can no longer be ignored. Rather it must be addressed regularly.

Stress is, and has always been, part of the human condition. However, we now know that chronic stress is common in virtually everyone's life, and millions of people the world over are suffering the physical effects of emotional stress. It doesn't have to be this way, which is why we feel this program is so important.

As you work your way through this course, you will find various ways to help yourself and others keep everyday stress in check, whether the cause is emotional, physical, or external. Nobody has all the answers because stress is personal and unique to the person who perceives it. Be assured, however, that the materials in this program have been researched and designed by the National Safety Council to give you the latest, most comprehensive approach to help you identify and control stress.

I hope you will absorb all you can from the enclosed lessons and then put the techniques into practice, beginning today. Above all, please take time to find a sense of personal balance in the course of each day, make stress management a part of your daily lifestyle, and plan now to live a longer, safer, and happier life by managing stress well.

Best wishes to you.

Sincerely,

T.C. Gilchrest
President
National Safety Council

Acknowledgments

Principal Author

Brian Luke Seaward, Ph.D.
The Center for Human Caring
Health Sciences Center
University of Colorado
Denver, CO

Principal Reviewers

Joan Cantwell
Supervisor
Health Services
Quaker Oats Company
Chicago, IL

Allen Elkin, Ph.D.
Director
Stress Management and Counseling Center
New York, NY

Gerald Elovitz, D.Ed.
Preventive Health Care Systems, Inc.
Hanover, MA

Andrea Frank
Director
Spiritual Wellness Network
Wauwatosa, WI

Anne Garlow
Director
Health & Fitness Center
Shaw, Pittman, Potts & Trowbridge
Washington, D.C.

Linda Gosselin
Massachusetts Emergency Care Training Agency
Millbury, MA

Barbara Rienzo, Ph.D.
Department of Health Science Education
University of Florida
Gainesville, FL

Larry Seidel, Senior Associate
Catholic Health Association
St. Louis, MO

Kenneth Steller, M.S., M.A.
Employee Health Services REAG
Aetna Life & Casualty
Hartford, CT

Alton Thygerson, Ph.D.
Department of Health Science
Brigham Young University
Provo, UT

Carol Vermilyea, Ph.D.
Project Manager
Johnson & Johnson Advanced Behavioral
    Technologies
New Brunswick, NJ

Marianne Vogt
Health Horizons Coordinator
DuPont Canada
Whitby, Ontario
Canada

Deitra Wengert, Ph.D., CHES
Associate Professor
School Health Education Coordinator
Department of Health Sciences
Towson State University
Towson, MD

Contents

Understanding the Nature of Stress

What Is Stress? • Stress in the Workplace • The Causes of Job Stress • Job Burnout

Workplace stress is truly epidemic.
—Northwestern National Life Insurance Co.

Recently, the concept of occupational stress has grabbed and shaken the national headlines. Why? Because an increasing number of disability claims are being based on "stress-related factors." As the pace of life increases, the advances of technology seem to outpace our ability to maintain productivity, and we feel as though we have little or no control. In essence, we become vulnerable to the occupational hazards of stress. Because we spend the greatest part of our waking day at the worksite *and* occupational stress is fast becoming a national health care issue, on-site stress management strategies are essential to help ensure optimal health for employees in every corner of the marketplace. Although we live in a more complex and hurried world than our ancestors did, we can survive and adapt to it. What this takes is daily recognition of our emotional barometer, effective strategies to deal with causes of stress, and relaxation skills to calm the body. We encourage you to use these stress management skills in your work environment as often as necessary to promote a greater sense of well-being.

What Is Stress?

We define stress as the inability to cope with a perceived threat to one's mental, physical, emotional, and spiritual well-being, which in time can affect one's physical health. Despite the different perspectives from which stress is observed, mental, emotional, physical, or spiritual, it is agreed that stress is our *perception* of the situation or circumstance in our environment. In other words, something that seems to be a threat to you might not even merit a second thought from one of your co-workers. Real or imagined, perceptions of stress are rooted in feelings of

Worksite stress, so prevalent in today's culture, can be offset by using effective stress management skills on a regular basis.

fear or anger. These feelings can be expressed as impatience, frustration, envy, hostility, depression, doubt, anxiety, guilt, worry, or apathy. At the worksite, these feelings can show up as pessimism, dissatisfaction, low productivity, and absenteeism. The result is that our stress-induced emotions, attitudes, and behaviors can lead to serious health problems. And it is a myth to think that only corporate executives who work 60+ hours a week are stressed. Tension can as easily come from boredom as from work overload.

Good Stress and Bad Stress

Not all stress is bad for you. In fact, many people agree that we need some degree of stress to stay

Worksite stress often results from feeling overwhelmed with responsibilities.

makes you angry, tense, confused, worried, guilty, or overwhelmed. Distress can take two forms: *acute stress* and *chronic stress*. Acute stress surfaces, is quite intense, and disappears quickly. For instance, trying to find a parking space at work, playing phone tag, and being late for a staff meeting are common examples. Chronic stressors, on the other hand, are not as intense, yet they seem to linger for days, weeks, or months. Examples of chronic stress might include financial problems, poor employer relations, and job burnout. It is the repeated wear and tear on the body from chronic stress that can have an adverse affect on your health and productivity. Ideally, a good stress management program is one in which you have enough stress to provide motivation and challenge to your job without the feeling of being overloaded.

No job is stress-free. In fact, every job comes with some degree of challenge and difficulty. Effective occupational stress management allows you to maintain a sense of self-control in your work setting so that any concerns that you encounter are perceived as *challenges,* not *threats.* But first, to fully understand effective stress management strategies, we need to review some basic concepts of the nature of stress.

healthy. But how can stress be good? When stress serves as a positive motivation, it is considered beneficial. Beyond this optimal point, stress does more harm than good. Actually, stress can be thought of in two ways: as *good stress* and *bad stress* (or *distress*). Good stress is referred to as positive stress: any situation or circumstance that you find motivating or inspiring. A job promotion and a paid vacation are examples of good stress. Usually, situations that are classified as good stress are enjoyable and, for this reason, are not considered to be a threat to your health. Bad stress, on the other hand, is that which

The Stress Response

The term *fight-or-flight response* was coined to describe the mechanisms involved with the body's response to survive a physical threat. Under stress, the body prepares itself for one of two types of action: *to fight* and defend oneself from the pursuing threat or *to run* and escape the ensuing danger. The fight response is triggered by anger. Conversely, the flight response is initiated by fear. Typically, either response includes a racing heart, rapid breathing, increased

Stressors can be either short term (finding a parking space) or long term (financial problems). It is the long-term stressors that seem to have the greatest consequence on our health.

2

Immediate Symptoms of the Stress Response

- Increased heart rate
- Increased blood pressure
- Increased muscle tension
- Increased perspiration
- Increased metabolic activity

sweating, increased muscle tension, and an increased metabolic rate. You might have noticed this response yourself if you have ever been stopped by a police officer for speeding. These symptoms do not go away until the threat is over (the police car drives off) and your body returns to a state of calmness. In the case of long-term stress, although not as pronounced, the body remains activated for quite some time. Eventually, various organs stop working properly.

Fight or Flight: An Outdated Survival Mechanism

We believe that the fight-or-flight response evolved primarily to counteract threats of a physical nature that endangered the lives of our early ancestors. Physical threats still exist, but we are often more troubled by threats of a mental, emotional, or spiritual nature. Despite the type of threat—whether it is corporate downsizing, several bounced checks, job burnout, or an episode of sexual harassment—your body reacts the same way. Because the stress response is activated by all types of perceived threats, not just physical danger, your body, like a car engine, can shift into overdrive while standing idle. If unchecked, the stress response can prove fatal.

Changes in heart rate, blood pressure, and muscle tension that are necessary to respond to physical dangers, such as a fire in the building, are quite *ineffective* in dealing with situations such as a 7:00 P.M. deadline, overtime with no pay, or inadequate child care. In other words, a racing heart and tense muscles won't help survive the job deadline any better.

Moreover, this stress response kicks in to the same degree and intensity, *even if the threat is imaginary* (sensations created in the depths of your mind, from the monsters hiding under your bed at age four to the suspicion that your boss is out to get you). In effect, the fight-or-flight response is an *antiquated mechanism*. The best way to update this system is to *respond rather than react*. We suggest making a habit of using effective coping and relaxation techniques so that you can minimize the effects of stress on your body and regain a sense of control in your life, especially at work, where you spend the greatest part of your day. These techniques will be explained in Chapters 3 and 4.

Stress in the Workplace

Stress in the workplace is not a new phenomenon. However, it has recently become a significant management problem in the business world. Corporate managers and industrial supervisors confide that stress has hit epidemic proportions, with two out of three employees admitting to feeling job stress. Current estimates indicate that job stress costs employers approximately $200 billion annually in absenteeism, tardiness, burnout, lower productivity, high turnover, worker's compensation, and rising health care insurance costs. It is now believed that as much as 80% of all disease and illness is initiated and aggravated by stress.

In a 1992 United Nations report, "job stress" was cited as *the* "20th-century disease," with three in five people stating that job stress is directly related to their acute and chronic health problems. In addition, the number of stress-related worker's compensation claims has risen sharply from those reported a decade ago. According to the International Labor Organization, 90% of these claims were successful. If for no other reason than a financial one, the issue of workplace stress has not gone unnoticed in corporate America. Today, managers are seeking ways to address and minimize the effects of job stress.

When a child's needs conflict with job responsibilities, parents experience stress.

Drawing by Modell; © 1985 The New Yorker Magazine, Inc.

I'd thank you Harrison, but, as you well know, yours is a thankless job.

The Causes of Job Stress

The reasons cited for job stress are many, ranging from changes in the economy to rapid advances in technology. Advances in technology, which were supposed to extend leisure time, now only add to the pressure to do more in less time. Typically, the average person spends between eight and twelve hours per day in the workplace. This is an increase of 163 hours per year since 1970 (not including travel time to and from work). Like machinists and secretaries, managers find that they, too, feel chained to the office. No matter what their job description, people find it difficult to separate themselves from their job now that fax machines, cellular car phones, beepers, and laptop computers are so common. Time spent in or near the workplace is not the only significant cause of employee stress. Additional reasons can be grouped into three categories: organizational, individual, and environmental causes.

Organizational Causes

- Lack of autonomy and creativity
- Unrealistic expectations, deadlines, and quotas
- Job relocation
- Inadequate training
- Stifled career
- Poor employer (supervisor) relations
- Keeping pace with technology (fax machines, voice mail, etc.)
- Downsizing, increased responsibilities without increased pay
- Employee victimization (reduction in benefits)

Individual Causes

- Juggling of career and family responsibilities
- Economic uncertainty
- Lack of appreciation and recognition of work
- Burnout, job dissatisfaction, boredom
- Inadequate childcare
- Conflict with co-workers

Environmental Causes

- Poor working conditions (lighting, noise, ventilation, temperature, etc.)
- Racial discrimination
- Sexual harassment
- Workplace violence
- Highway traffic to and from work

Job Burnout

Job burnout is perhaps the most common result of occupational stress. Typical symptoms of job burnout include boredom, depression, pessimism, lack of concentration, poor work quality, dissatisfaction, absenteeism, and illness. Although work overload is cited as the most common reason for job burnout, job boredom is equally likely to promote feelings of occupational exhaustion. In either case, employees feel as though they have little or no control of factors at the worksite. A mental surrender to this situation may lead to symptoms of illness and disease.

The irony of worksite stress is that it is considered a taboo subject to discuss with supervisors. Workers openly admit that they are afraid they will lose their job or be denied a promotion if they openly blame their health or work performance on job stress. Thousands of workers confide that stress overload can be looked on as a sign of weakness, vulnerability, and low job security. Even employees who feel that they can control their stress may find themselves face to face with a unique American phenomenon: the disgruntled employee. Research compiled at Northeastern University now shows that situations involving disgruntled employees who take revenge on fellow co-workers and employers occur twice every month in the United States. Predictions suggest that this number is likely to rise sharply throughout the 1990s and beyond.

It is now known that while all jobs can promote tension, some occupations seem more likely to produce stress than others. The following are considered the most stressful careers:

Stress-Producing Jobs

postal workers	nurses
stockbrokers	customer service
journalists	personnel
airline pilots	waiters and waitresses
middle managers	inner-city teachers
secretaries	miners
police officers	air traffic controllers
advertising	firefighters
executives	paramedics
medical interns	

• EXERCISE 1 •

Identifying Your Stressors

One of the first goals in stress management is to increase your awareness of your thoughts, feelings, and perceptions. To begin this series of workbook exercises, we recommend that you make a list of your top ten current stressors. Try to identify those things at work that worry, upset, or frustrate you. List them according to the following categories. As with all these workbook exercises, this is confidential.

List Your Top Ten Stressors

	Organizational Causes	Individual Causes	Environmental Causes
1.			
2.			
3.			
4.			
5.			
6.			
7.			
8.			
9.			
10.			

Personal Stress Scale

On a scale of 0–10 (0 = no stress, 10 = maximal stress/burnout), rate where you feel your current occupational stress level is.

1   2   3   4   5   6   7   8   9   10

• EXERCISE 2 •
Job Stress Profile

The following personal and confidential quiz is from the American Institute of Stress and is designed to help determine your own level of workplace stress. Please take a few minutes to rank each of the ten questions, on a sliding scale from 1 to 10, as follows:

1 if you strongly disagree with the statement.
10 if you strongly agree with the statement.

Work Stress Survey

_____ 1. At work, I can't say what I really think or get things off my chest.

_____ 2. My job has a lot of responsibilities, but I don't have much authority or autonomy.

_____ 3. I could usually do a much better job if I had more time.

_____ 4. I seldom receive adequate acknowledgment or appreciation when my work is really good.

_____ 5. In general, I'm not particularly proud of my job or satisfied with my job.

_____ 6. I think that I'm repeatedly picked on while at work.

_____ 7. My workplace environment is not very pleasant or particularly safe.

_____ 8. My job interferes with my family, social obligations, and personal needs.

_____ 9. I tend to have frequent arguments with my supervisors, co-workers, or customers.

_____ 10. Most of the time, I feel that I have little control over my life at work.

TOTAL

_____ Please add up the number you gave each question. Total your job stress score.

Legend for your job stress score:

10–29 = low job stress

30–50 = moderate job stress

51–75 = high job stress

76–100 = VERY HIGH job stress; professional counseling may be needed

Source: Wallace, Jean, "Reduce Job Stress Before It Reduces You." In *Health and Safety,* November 1992. Reprinted courtesy of Occupational Health and Safety.

Negative Effects of Stress

Emotional Stress • Physical Effects of Stress

> *Thoughts become chemicals. They can kill or cure.*
> —Bernie Siegel, M.D.

Emotional Stress

As we mentioned in Chapter 1, stress begins with a perception of some information gathered by one or more of our five senses. No sooner does the brain receive this information than it is paired with an emotional response, usually some expression or anger or fear. If left unresolved, these emotions can promote a sense of fatigue, alienation, and possibly depression. We can become quite vulnerable to stressful perceptions when our self-esteem is low, and not surprisingly, a critical mass of stress can lower our self-esteem. The result is a difficult cycle to break. The following are some ways in which emotional stress can surface as a result of occupational overload and job burnout. In addition, we also offer some tips to help break the stress-related low-self-esteem cycle.

Fatigue

Under stress, our bodies are activated to the fight-or-flight response, whether we choose to move or remain still. The result is that we expend more energy, and this can cause both mental and physical fatigue. When several stressors beg for our attention, such as deadlines, productivity records, or staff meetings, the following can happen:

1. Our focus on work is divided.
2. Our attention span is reduced.
3. Our ability to retain information is greatly limited.
4. Our decision-making process is significantly compromised.

Many times, our thoughts become magnified and distorted, making mountains out of molehills. This too can make us feel overwhelmed with our jobs. All of these factors can lead to mental and emotional fatigue. Over time, we can begin to lose interest in our work and become less motivated. Ultimately, the quality of work and the quality of life suffer.

Alienation

When people sense a loss of control in their job and when they begin to feel taken advantage of by employers, co-workers, or the company they work for, feelings of alienation, isolation, and victimization surface. If unchecked and unresolved, these perceptions validate feelings of anger and frustration. As a result, anger can be expressed as insensitivity toward co-workers, cynicism, and even hostility. Unresolved or mismanaged anger can surface in one of four ways: (1) hostility (exploders), (2) guilt (self-punishers), (3) revenge (underhanders), and (4) suppression (somatizers, in whom physical symptoms of stress appear such as migraine headaches, ulcers, or hypertension). Unresolved anger only increases a sense of isolation and alienation at the work environment.

Depression

People who constantly feel a loss of control (either overwhelmed or bored) in their work environment may end up with feelings of depression. If you feel unhappy with your current situation but unable to leave your job for a variety of reasons, you might succumb to feelings of depression through a sense of hopelessness. Not only might feelings of depression affect the quality of your work, they can also suppress the immune system, making you more vulnerable to disease and illness.

Low Self-Esteem

Self-esteem is often described as a sense of self-worth and self-acceptance. It is reflected in the things we say, the clothes we wear, and perhaps most evidently in our behaviors. In the North American culture, which is so strongly influenced by the Puritan work ethic in which "worth equals work," self-esteem

Components of Self-Esteem

Self-esteem is thought to be comprised of these four components.

- **Connectedness**   A feeling of bonding and acceptance from your friends, peers, and colleagues and a sense of satisfaction that your relationships are significant and nurturing and affirmed by others.
- **Uniqueness**   A feeling that you hold qualities that make you special and different and that these qualities are respected and admired by others as well as yourself.
- **Empowerment**   A sense that you can access your inner resources to create new opportunities and use your resources and capabilities to gain and keep a sense of control in your life.
- **Models**   People whom you admire for certain characteristics that you would like to enhance in yourself and whom you use as mentors to reach your highest potential.

often seems tied solely to one's occupational status, work productivity, or paycheck. When occupational stress hits a critical level, your self-esteem can crumble. People with low self-esteem generate feelings of powerlessness, frustration, depression, and victimization. Whereas people with low self-esteem are especially susceptible to the pressures of stress, people with high self-esteem display confidence and enthusiasm and tolerate frustration well. Because a strong sense of self-esteem is critical to effective stress reduction, the primary goal in stress management programs is to help people develop and nurture high self-esteem. The four basic elements that comprise self-esteem are connectedness, uniqueness, empowerment, and models. All of these factors need to be present and cultivated throughout your life to ensure a sense of high self-esteem.

Tips for Raising Self-Esteem at Work

1. **Disarm your negative critic:** Challenge the voice inside your head that feeds your conscious mind with put-downs and negative comments. Tell yourself that you are doing a good job on the job. A critic with only a negative side is unbalanced and dangerous to your self-esteem. Then . . .

2. **Give yourself positive reinforcements and affirmations:** Remind yourself of your good qualities (e.g., I am a lovable person). Write these down, and look at the list and repeat these to yourself often in the course of a day.

3. **Avoid "should haves":** Don't place a guilt trip on yourself for unmet expectations. Learn from the past, but don't dwell on it. Look for new opportunities for growth.

4. **Focus on those qualities that make you special:** Explore your own identity, and do not place all your self-worth in a paycheck.

5. **Avoid comparing yourself to others:** Respect your own uniqueness, and learn to cultivate it. At the same time, ask yourself who your role models are and how the traits that you admire in them can be fostered in yourself.

6. **Diversify your interests:** Don't put all your eggs in one basket. Diversify so that if one aspect of your life (work) becomes troubled, other areas (e.g., a hobby, family) can compensate to keep you afloat.

7. **Strengthen your connectedness:** Widen your network of friends and your connection with special places that recharge your energy and strengthen your bonds throughout your environment. Nurture these relationships.

8. **Avoid self-victimization:** Martyrs are often admired, but begging for pity and sympathy gets old, and the effects are short-lived.

9. **Reassert yourself and your value before and during a stressful event:** High self-esteem is consid-

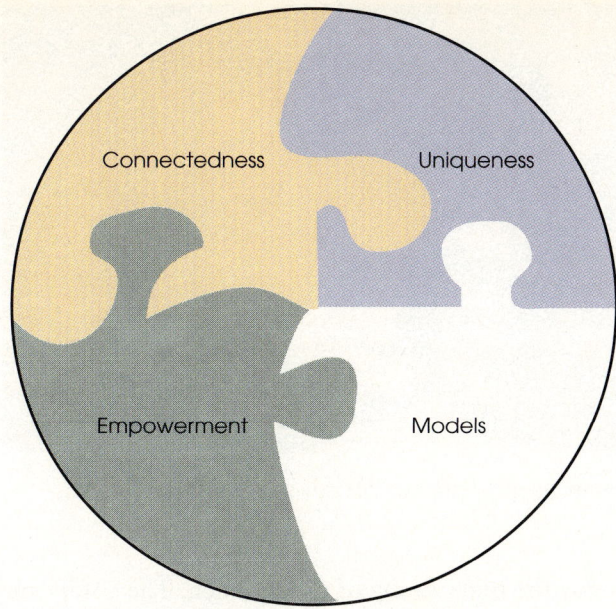

Components of Self-Esteem

Having a sense of connectedness with people you work with as part of your social support network with is paramount to high self-esteem.

Hobbies serve not only to help build self-esteem, they actually help nurture one's sense of creativity, which often transfers back to problem-solving techniques at work.

ered the best defense against stress, since successful strategies used to combat stress are useless without a strong feeling of self-worth and self-value. Although quite abstract, your self-esteem should be attended to regularly (every day) like brushing your teeth and eating. It *is* important!!!

Physical Effects of Stress

The association between stress and disease is not a new one. For centuries, doctors have suspected that emotions can significantly affect one's health. In the early 1970s, it was suggested that up to 60% of all disease and illness was stress-related. In light of recent findings about the mind-body interaction, current estimates predict that as many as 80% of all health-related problems are either caused or made worse by stress. The list of such disorders is nearly endless, from the common cold to cancer. Now, science has proved what was known intuitively: Emotions can either help or hinder the immune system, thereby affecting your health.

To understand the relationship between stress and disease, it is important to know that several factors must come together to create or aggravate an illness. These include, but are not limited to, stress-promoting attitudes and their effects on the nervous system, the hormonal system, and the immune system.

At first, it was noted that the repeated rush of hormones released in the fight-or-flight response targeted specific organs to go into dysfunction. Then it was discovered that these same stress hormones actually "eat up" white blood cells, thereby lowering your resistance to disease and illness. While these factors have been found to be true, we have now learned through various studies that the human body is more complicated than was once thought. In fact, now we know that there is a direct link between our emotions and the functions of white blood cells that bypasses the nervous and hormonal system altogether. The work of Norman Cousins, Dr. Bernie Siegel, Dr. Deepak Chopra, Joan Borysenko, and Dr. Larry Dossey, among others, has shown us that, indeed, our physical health is truly a reflection of our emotional health.

The following are some of the more common disorders that are now known to be related to chronic stress directly tied to the functions of the ner-

Positive Affirmation Statements

1. Damn, I'm good.
2. I am filled with happiness.
3. Love is the answer.
4. I am calm and relaxed.
5. I have confidence in myself.
6. I am an important piece of the whole.
7. I am a lovable person.
8. I radiate success!
9. I am worthy of being loved.
10. Your positive affirmation statement:
   _____.

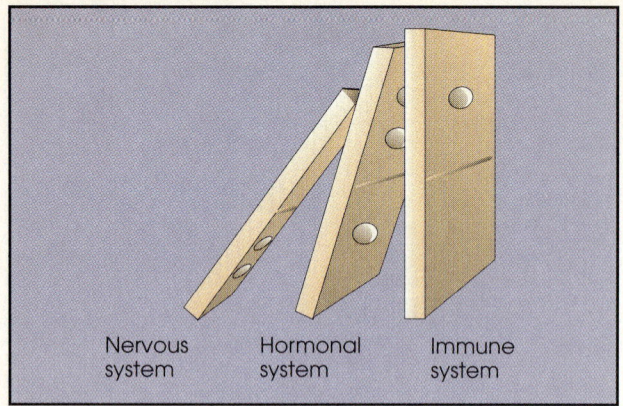

Three symbolic dominoes representing the body's reaction to physiological stress.

Headaches are an obvious symptom of stress.

vous system, the hormonal system, or the immune system. All of these illnesses have been shown to be significantly affected by a variety of relaxation techniques (see Chapter 4).

Aches and Pains

Tension Headaches Muscle tension is the number one symptom of stress. It is most likely to appear as tension headaches, a clenched jaw, a stiff neck, and lower back pain. The most common of these, tension headaches, are produced by muscle contractions of the forehead, eyes, neck, and jaw. Most people are unaware of increased muscle tension until pain begins in the front of the head.

Migraine Headaches A migraine headache is caused by an increased blood flow and chemical secretions to the head. Symptoms can include a flash of light followed by intense throbbing, dizziness, and nausea. It is interesting to note that migraines do not occur in the midst of a stressor, but rather hours later. In many cases, migraines are thought to be related to the inability to express anger and frustration.

Temporomandibular Joint Dysfunction (TMJ) Repeated contraction of the jaw muscles (often during sleep) can lead to a problem called temporomandibular joint dysfunction (TMJ). Other symptoms include muscle pain, clicking or popping sounds when chewing, and tension headaches and earaches. Like migraines, TMJ is thought to be associated with the inability to express feelings of anger.

Stomach Troubles

Ulcers and Colitis Ulcers are caused by an excess secretion of digestive fluids, which inflame and de-

stroy the inner lining of the stomach. The colon, situated below the stomach (along the gastrointestinal track), is also prone to ulceration, producing colitis (an inflammation of the inner lining of the colon). Stress in the form of anxiety is though to be strongly associated with this.

Irritable Bowel Syndrome Irritable bowel syndrome (IBS) is characterized by repeated bouts of abdominal pain or tenderness, cramps, diarrhea, nausea, constipation, and excessive gas. While symptoms may vary from person to person, this stress-related disorder is most commonly associated with anxiety and depression.

Nervous Anxiety

Insomnia The inability to sleep is a sure symptom of an overactive nervous system. Excess neural stimulation to the brain and muscle tissue can cause

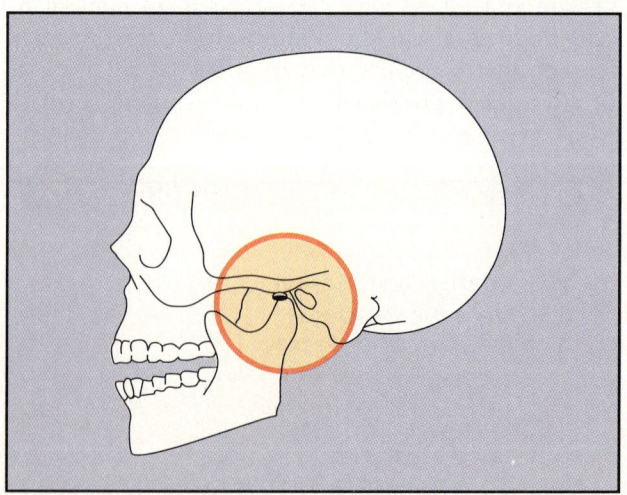

The mandibular joint can be a target of stress, causing temporomandibular joint dysfunction (TMJ).

much restlessness in the day or night, all of which is related to nervous anxiety.

Bronchial Asthma   The bronchioles are tubes that carry air into the lungs. During an asthma attack, the tubes begin to swell up with bronchial fluid. Soon the person feels as though he or she is choking and cannot breathe. Asthmatic attacks can be severe enough to place a person in the hospital and in some cases are even fatal. Asthmatic attacks are often linked with anxiety.

Allergies   An allergic reaction is initiated when a foreign substance such as pollen or dust enters the body. However, pollenlike substances are not necessary to trigger an allergic reaction. The mere memory of an attack can trigger the symptoms. It is now known that allergic reactions are more prevalent and severe when subjects are prone to anxiety. Over-the-counter medications (containing antihistamines) and allergy shots are the most common approach to dealing with allergies. Relaxation techniques also minimize the effects of these foreign substances.

Rheumatoid Arthritis   Rheumatoid arthritis, a joint and connective tissue disease, occurs when joints swell, causing the joint tissue to become inflamed. With time, fluid may actually enter the cartilage and bone tissue, causing further deterioration of the joint. There is speculation that rheumatoid arthritis has a genetic link as well as an association with stress. Typically, the severity of arthritic pain is re-

The list of allergy-producing substances is nearly endless. Pollen and dust are two of the most common ones.

lated to episodes of stress, particularly to suppressed anger.

Diseases

The Common Cold and Influenza   It is no coincidence that the occasions when we are most stressed are the times when we are the most likely to catch a cold. When our immune defenses are down, we are more likely to succumb to nearby viruses. Current findings support the notion that colds are definitely related to undue stress.

Coronary Heart Disease   Two factors link the stress response to the development of coronary heart disease. The first is high blood pressure, or *hypertension* (> 145/90 mm Hg.) High blood pressure is known to produce damage to the inner lining of the coronary vessels that supply the heart muscle with oxygen. The second link involves the release of *cortisol* from the adrenal gland, which is known to increase levels of cholesterol in the blood. Cholesterol acts as a bandage to repair damaged vessel walls. Unfortunately, it ultimately causes more damage to the arteries, blocking the passage of blood.

There are three stages of coronary heart disease: First, a fatty streak appears along the lining of the vessel wall; next, there is a thickening of the plaque build-up; finally, the arteries harden like lead pipes.

Cancer   Cancer affects one out of every four Americans. The American Cancer Society defines cancer as "a large group of diseases all characterized by uncontrolled growth and spread of abnormal cells." When normal cells mutate to abnormal cells, the body treats them as a foreign substance. One function of white blood cells is to search out and destroy mutant cells. If for some reason the number of white

Insomnia is a common symptom of chronic work-related stressors.

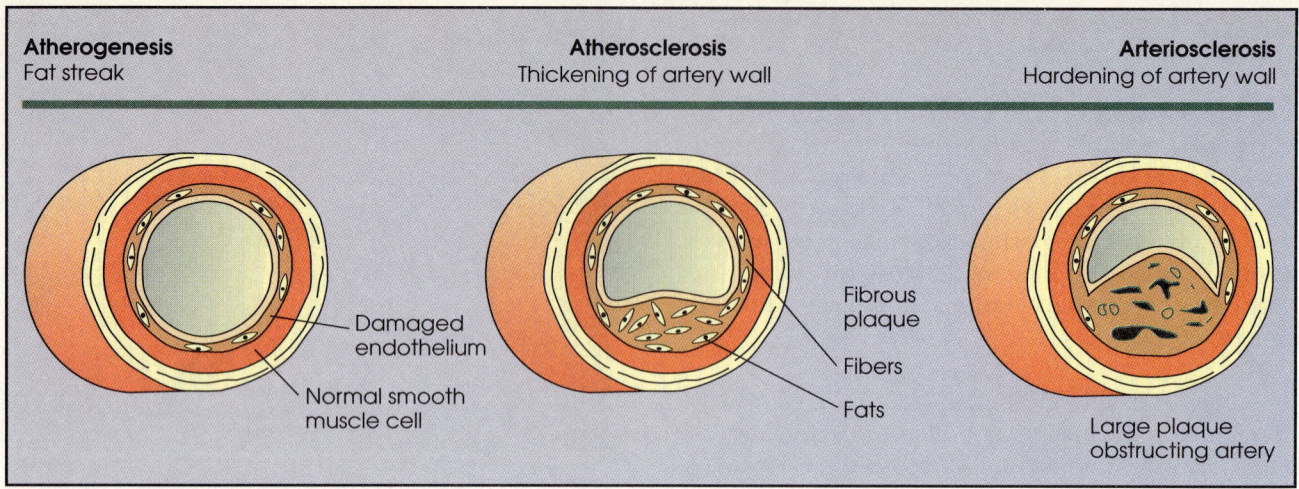

Atherogenesis
Fat streak

Atherosclerosis
Thickening of artery wall

Arteriosclerosis
Hardening of artery wall

Damaged endothelium

Normal smooth muscle cell

Fibrous plaque

Fibers

Fats

Large plaque obstructing artery

Coronary heart disease can start as early as age five, causing damage to the inner lining of artery walls. Cholesterol deposits, which attempt to heal damaged tissue, actually thicken the passage, thus decreasing the diameter of the vessel for blood circulation. The greater the thickness, the greater the blockage to that vessel, the more pressure is needed to circulate blood, and thus the greater the chance of a heart attack or stroke.

Seven Warning Signs of Cancer

The following is a list of the seven major warning signs for cancer issued by the American Cancer Society:

1. **C**hange in bowel or bladder habits
2. **A** sore that does not heal
3. **U**nusual bleeding or discharge
4. **T**hickening or lump in breast, testicles, or elsewhere
5. **I**ndigestion or difficulty swallowing
6. **O**bvious changes in warts, moles, or other skin markings
7. **N**agging cough or hoarseness

If any of these persist for a period of five days, see a physician immediately.

Source: Used with permission. © American Cancer Society, Inc.

blood cells is too low, then an abnormal cell may go undetected, and the likelihood of a tumor increases. Research suggests that the body produces about six mutant cells per day. Under normal conditions, white blood cells can do their job well. Under stressful conditions, mutant cells can go undetected and become cancerous tumors. Negative emotions appear to suppress the number of white blood cells, thereby increasing the risk for cancer tumors to grow. (We would like to point out that there is still much to be discovered about the relationship between stress and cancer.)

• EXERCISE 1 •
Anger Recognition Checklist

The following is a quick exercise to help you understand how anger can surface in the course of a working day and how you may mismanage it. Put a check mark in front of any of the following that apply to you when you get angry. Next, if applicable, try to identify your most common mismanaged anger style.

_____ anxious

_____ depressed

_____ overeat

_____ start dieting

_____ trouble sleeping

_____ excessive sleeping

_____ careless driving

_____ chronic fatigue

_____ abuse alcohol/drugs

_____ explode in rage

_____ cold withdrawal

_____ headaches

_____ sarcasm

_____ hostile joking

_____ accident-prone

_____ guilty and self-blaming

_____ high blood pressure

_____ frequent nightmares

_____ harp/nag

_____ intellectualize

_____ stomach upsets
   (e.g., gas, cramps, colitis)

_____ muscle tension
   (e.g., shoulders, leg, fist)

_____ name-call

_____ cry

_____ threaten others

_____ buy things

_____ frequent lateness

_____ never feel angry

_____ tight, clenched jaw

_____ bored

_____ nausea, vomiting

_____ skin eruptions

_____ easily irritable

_____ sexual difficulties

_____ backache

_____ busy work
   (e.g., clean, straighten)

_____ sulk, whine

_____ hit, throw things

Mismanaged Anger Styles
When I mismanage my anger, I typically express myself in the following way (check one):

_____ 1. Exploder

_____ 2. Self-punisher (guilt)

_____ 3. Underhander (revenge, sarcasm)

_____ 4. Somatizer (suppress anger feelings)

My average number of anger episodes per day is _____.

Reprinted with permission from Gloria Mog, L.C.S.W. Psychiatric Associates of Greater Washington D.C.

• EXERCISE 2 •
Self-Esteem Appraisal

On the basis of what you know and what you have read about self-esteem, how would you rate your level of self-esteem in the following areas (0 = low, 10 = extremely high)?

Overall Self-Esteem (All Factors Considered):

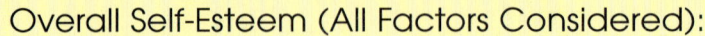
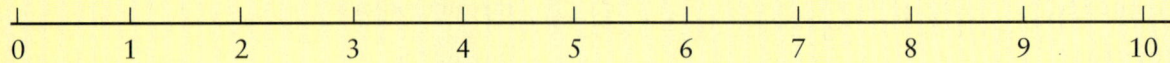

| 0 | 1 | 2 | 3 | 4 | 5 | 6 | 7 | 8 | 9 | 10 |

Present Level of Self-Esteem:

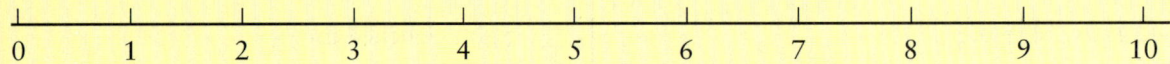

| 0 | 1 | 2 | 3 | 4 | 5 | 6 | 7 | 8 | 9 | 10 |

Professional (Career) Self-Esteem:

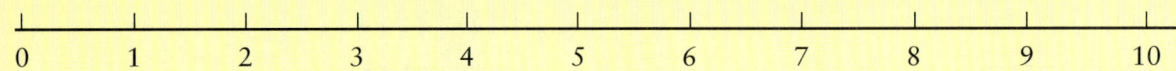

| 0 | 1 | 2 | 3 | 4 | 5 | 6 | 7 | 8 | 9 | 10 |

As discussed in this chapter, self-esteem is thought to comprise four components: connectedness, uniqueness, empowerment, and models. With respect to these four areas, let's take a look at your level of overall self-esteem. Try to answer these questions as best you can.

A. As we will see in Chapter 3, social support groups are thought to be crucial to one's health status. To have a sense of belonging is very important in one's life. To whom (and this can include animals) do you feel you have a sense of belonging? Briefly describe why.
   1.
   2.
   3.
   4.
   5.

B. List five things about yourself that make you feel special and unique.
   1.
   2.
   3.
   4.
   5.

C. List five areas or aspects of your life in which you feel that you are in control or are self-empowered.
   1.
   2.
   3.
   4.
   5.

D. Who are your role models or mentors? Name five people who have one or more characteristics that you wish to emulate, include, or strengthen as part of your own personality, and describe those characteristics.
   1.
   2.
   3.
   4.
   5.

• **EXERCISE 3** •

Physical Symptom Questionnaire

Look over the following list of stress-related symptoms, and circle how often they have occurred in the past week, how severe they seemed to you, and how long they lasted. Then reflect back on the past week's workload, and see whether you notice any connection.

	How Often (number of days in the past week)	How Severe (1 = mild, 5 = severe)	How Long (1 = 1 hour, 5 = all day)
1. Tension headache	0 1 2 3 4 5 6 7	1 2 3 4 5	1 2 3 4 5
2. Migraine headache	0 1 2 3 4 5 6 7	1 2 3 4 5	1 2 3 4 5
3. Muscle tension (neck and/or shoulders)	0 1 2 3 4 5 6 7	1 2 3 4 5	1 2 3 4 5
4. Muscle tension (lower back)	0 1 2 3 4 5 6 7	1 2 3 4 5	1 2 3 4 5
5. Joint pain	0 1 2 3 4 5 6 7	1 2 3 4 5	1 2 3 4 5
6. Cold	0 1 2 3 4 5 6 7	1 2 3 4 5	1 2 3 4 5
7. Flu	0 1 2 3 4 5 6 7	1 2 3 4 5	1 2 3 4 5
8. Stomachache	0 1 2 3 4 5 6 7	1 2 3 4 5	1 2 3 4 5
9. Stomach/abdominal bloating/distention gas	0 1 2 3 4 5 6 7	1 2 3 4 5	1 2 3 4 5
10. Diarrhea	0 1 2 3 4 5 6 7	1 2 3 4 5	1 2 3 4 5
11. Constipation	0 1 2 3 4 5 6 7	1 2 3 4 5	1 2 3 4 5
12. Ulcer flare-up	0 1 2 3 4 5 6 7	1 2 3 4 5	1 2 3 4 5
13. Asthma attack	0 1 2 3 4 5 6 7	1 2 3 4 5	1 2 3 4 5
14. Allergies	0 1 2 3 4 5 6 7	1 2 3 4 5	1 2 3 4 5
15. Canker/cold sores	0 1 2 3 4 5 6 7	1 2 3 4 5	1 2 3 4 5
16. Dizzy spells	0 1 2 3 4 5 6 7	1 2 3 4 5	1 2 3 4 5
17. Heart palpitations (racing heart)	0 1 2 3 4 5 6 7	1 2 3 4 5	1 2 3 4 5
18. TMJ	0 1 2 3 4 5 6 7	1 2 3 4 5	1 2 3 4 5
19. Insomnia	0 1 2 3 4 5 6 7	1 2 3 4 5	1 2 3 4 5
20. Nightmares	0 1 2 3 4 5 6 7	1 2 3 4 5	1 2 3 4 5
21. Fatigue	0 1 2 3 4 5 6 7	1 2 3 4 5	1 2 3 4 5
22. Hemorrhoids	0 1 2 3 4 5 6 7	1 2 3 4 5	1 2 3 4 5
23. Pimples/acne	0 1 2 3 4 5 6 7	1 2 3 4 5	1 2 3 4 5
24. Cramps	0 1 2 3 4 5 6 7	1 2 3 4 5	1 2 3 4 5
25. Frequent accidents	0 1 2 3 4 5 6 7	1 2 3 4 5	1 2 3 4 5
26. Other (please specify)	0 1 2 3 4 5 6 7	1 2 3 4 5	1 2 3 4 5

Score: Take a look at the entire list. Do you observe any patterns or relationships between your stress levels and your physical health? A value over 30 points may indicate a stress-related health problem. If it seems to you that these symptoms are related to undue stress, they probably are. While medical treatment is advocated where necessary, the regular use of relaxation techniques may lessen the intensity, frequency, and duration of these episodes.

3

Effective Coping Skills

Personal Coping Skills • Interpersonal Coping Skills

There is no such thing as a problem without a gift for you in its hands. You seek problems because you need their gifts.

—Richard Bach, *Illusions*

To effectively deal with occupational stress, no matter how big or small the problem, a coping strategy is needed. There are many types of coping strategies, but not all of them are effective. Most ineffective coping strategies fall under the domain of *avoidance,* and these are reflected in our current national health problems: alcohol and drug abuse, battered spouses and children, hostile aggression, social violence, and suicide. Effective coping strategies, on the other hand, work toward a peaceful resolution. In most cases, the coping skills that we use seem like second nature to us. But as the number and intensity of our stressors increase, routine coping strategies often fail to do an effective job. The result can be that we feel physically exhausted, mentally paralyzed, and emotionally drained. All of these factors result in poor work productivity.

We define effective coping as the mental process of managing demands that are appraised as a challenge to one's resources. In this case, coping requires both internal and external resources. Creativity, patience, optimism, intuition, a sense of humor, willpower, and compassion are examples of internal resources. External resources include time, money, and social support.

Coping strategies that successfully deal with stress involve four basic components:

1. **Increased awareness of the problem:** A clear, objective focus and a full perspective on the situation at hand.
2. **Information processing:** An approach that includes a shift in your perception in order to *deactivate* the threat. Information processing also includes gathering information and assessing all resources available in order to resolve the problem.
3. **Changing behaviors:** Consciously chosen actions that, combined with a positive attitude, dissolve, minimize, or eradicate the stressor.
4. **Peaceful resolution:** A feeling that the situation has successfully been brought to closure.

Effective Coping Strategies = Increased Awareness +

Information Processing + Modified Behavior

+ Peaceful Resolution

The goal of effective coping skills is not merely to survive at work, but to thrive in the face of adversity. Is there a relationship between the use of effective coping strategies and personality at the worksite? Some researchers think so. People who exhibit stress-prone personality traits (e.g., Type A behavior [hostile anger], codependency, and helpless/hopeless behaviors) are more likely to choose and employ negative coping styles by avoiding the problem and claiming victimization from their stressors. People who exhibit stress-resistant personality traits (confidence and high self-esteem) are more likely to see challenges rather than threats, take calculated risks, diplomatically confront rather than avoid problems, and quickly resolve their stressors.

In the work environment, a single coping technique is rarely used alone. Rather, several skills are used *collectively* to build a stronger defense against stress. Among the many coping strategies that can make you more aware of how to understand and deal with your problems are reframing, information seeking, creative problem solving, journal writing, and humor therapy. Other coping skills emphasize a thinking strategy combined with a conscious change in behavior. These include time management, assertiveness skills, communication skills, and social engineering. Like learning to use a personal computer or improving your bowling score, coping skills improve with practice. It is important to remember that no one coping technique will work as a defense against all types of stress. This is why it is important to have many coping skills to choose from to make your life less stressful. We have divided this section into two parts: personal coping skills and interpersonal coping skills.

Personal Coping Skills

Reframing Stressful Thoughts

Multiple deadlines. A disgruntled customer. Busy phone lines. Repeated interruptions. Stressors come in all shapes and sizes. We now know that it is not the circumstance or environment that is stressful, but rather the perception or interpretation of the situation. If the perception is negative, it can become both a mental and physical liability. Whatever the event, perceptions can become magnified and distorted entirely out of proportion to their real size, turning everyday problems into catastrophic monsters.

Toxic Thoughts   Each of us has a never-ending conversation running through our head. This dialogue is called *self-talk*. As with a radio, we have the option to select among several stations; however, we tend to tune into the station with the negative format. Most self-talk consists of negative thoughts, criticisms, and put-downs, or what are now referred to as *toxic thoughts*. Toxic thoughts are directly related to low self-esteem.

Toxic thoughts are often the result of low self-esteem. Furthermore, they perpetuate the cycle of low

Toxic Thoughts

Toxic thoughts can appear in the following ways:

1. **Pessimism:** Casting a negative perspective on almost every situation.
2. **Catastrophizing:** Making the worst of a situation, always seeing everything as awful.
3. **Blaming:** Shifting the responsibility of circumstances to someone other than yourself.
4. **Perfectionism:** Imposing yourself or others to above-human standards, making everything you do perfect.
5. **Polarized thinking:** An attitude by which everything is seen at extremes, either good or bad, black or white) with no middle ground.
6. **Should-ing:** Reprimanding yourself for things you "should have" done.
7. **Victimization:** An attitude that makes you feel as though you have been singled out by other people, events, or circumstances and taken advantage of.

self-esteem by ignoring or destroying feelings of self-worth and self-acceptance. Negative thoughts are actually a response that we learn in childhood and carry into our adult lives. Studies show that a pessimistic attitude that generates toxic thoughts also makes us more prone to disease and illness. On the other hand, an optimistic attitude promotes a great sense of well-being. In short, toxic thoughts can have a toxic effect on the body and put our health at risk. For example, from studies looking at the longevity of cancer patients with breast cancer, we learn that patients with a fighting spirit are more likely to live longer than those who appear to give in and give up. (Every documented case of a miracle cure has been accompanied by a positive change in attitude.) Furthermore, our negative thoughts influence negative actions in what

Whether stress is imaginary or real, it can cause a stress response in the body.

It is normal to have negative thoughts, but too many too often can result in a pessimistic outlook, which only attracts more stress.

thinking that can block the path to resolution. Tools to initiate the reframing process and dismantle the obstacles include the use of humor, positive affirmations, and creativity. One major element of the reframing process that is designed to bolster self-esteem is the use of positive affirmations (e.g., "I am confident" or "I am doing the best I can"). Confidence building in the form of positive self-talk can counterbalance the voice of the "inner critic," the voice in our head that constantly tells us we're just not good enough.

A Humorous Outlook   Ever since Norman Cousins laughed himself back to health from a life-threatening disease in 1964, the use of humor or comic relief has been widely recognized as a means to effectively cope with stress. On the average, Americans laugh fifteen times per day, yet under chronic stress, this number can be as low as zero. The use of humor can help relieve the tension of anger when we can take a moment to laugh at our misfortunes and mistakes. Humor can be used to dilute our sense of fear as well. Humor therapists agree that humor, like stress, is a perception. When we attempt to look at the humorous side of life, we tend to in-

is called the *self-fulfilling prophecy*. Quite often, stubbornness and the comfort of our own opinions become obstacles to the reframing process. Think of how you can change the dialogue in your mind so that you produce fewer toxic thoughts in the workplace.

Adopting a Positive Attitude   Reframing is a coping technique that changes a stressful attitude to a less threatening perception—in other words, from a negative, self-defeating attitude to a positive one. *In every moment, we choose the attitude that we find ourselves in.* The purpose of reframing is to widen our perspective and focus on the positive aspects of challenging situations. The ability to see more than what is directly in front of you is not merely a poetic expression. It has been proven that your field of vision actually narrows under stress. When your vision is limited, so too are the possibilities for dealing with the situation.

Reframing should not be confused with rationalization. Rationalization is an ego defense mechanism in which you make excuses and blame others, shifting the responsibility away from yourself toward someone or something else. Reframing allows you to find and adopt a positive mind frame to deal with any unpleasant situation involving your work. Reframing does not deny you the ability to mourn, grieve, or experience negative thoughts that result from stress. Nor is reframing a "Pollyanna" attitude. It does, however, allow you to break the cycle of negative

"It's a fax from your dog, Mr. Dansworth. It looks like your cat."

Humor is an effective means of reducing tension and coping with stress.

oculate ourselves from the hazards of stressful perceptions. It is important to remember, when a humorous approach is used, that it not be self-deprecating to lower your own self-esteem, nor should humor, particularly sarcasm, be used to direct anger at others. Think of some ways in which you can use elements of humor to lift your spirits at the office to hit your daily quota of fifteen humorous moments.

Acceptance, an Alternative Mind Frame We often encounter situations that we cannot control: a manipulative boss, impossible deadlines, an obnoxious co-worker, or corporate layoffs. The reality of the situation is not pleasant at the lightest of moments. But, like pushing water uphill, we tend to waste a lot of personal energy trying to change things over which we have no control. The economy and behavior of co-workers are two examples. When you have absolutely no control over a situation, accept it as it is and move on. There is a fine balance between control and acceptance, and acceptance should not be confused with apathy or surrender. Let there be no doubt, acceptance is perhaps the hardest frame of mind to adopt. And acceptance does not happen overnight. It is an attitude that may take days, weeks, even months to adopt, given the nature of the stressor, but in some cases it is the only choice.

Steps to Initiate Reframing The following are suggested for using reframing as a coping technique. Think of a situation at work and try this four-step approach:

1. **Increase your awareness:** Identify your stressor by asking yourself what it is that is bothering you (refer to Exercise 1 in Chapter 1). This may include writing down what is on your mind, including all your fears, frustrations, and worries.

2. **Reframe your perception:** Create a positive reference toward this one circumstance by finding something positive about the situation.

3. **Adopt this new attitude:** Try to focus on the positive and minimize the negative aspects of the problem.

4. **Evaluate:** Make an assessment of your new attitude, and ask yourself, "Did this help?" If it turns out that this was a complete failure, then go back to the cause of the problem and find something else about the situation that is positive. Even the worst situations offer valuable lessons. If we take the time to learn these lessons, then every stressor has a positive aspect.

Some Additional Tips for Reframing

1. **Disarm the negative critic:** Stop the negative conversation in your head. When you become aware of your negative self-talk, say to yourself, "Stop this

thought," and then focus your attention on one of your positive attributes.

2. **Take responsibility for your own thoughts:** If you find yourself blaming others for events that make you feel hurt, ask yourself how you can turn this blame into personal responsibility for your own thoughts and feelings without feeling guilty.

3. **Fine-tune expectations:** Many times we walk into situations with a preconceived attitude of how it should be. When these expectations are not met to our satisfaction, then negative feelings are generated. Fine-tuning expectations doesn't mean abandoning your ideals. Rather, it means running your perceptions through a reality check, questioning their validity, and allowing them to match the given situation.

4. **Give yourself positive affirmations:** Positive affirmations (e.g., "I am a lovable person" or "I can do it") balance the internal conversation with good thoughts to enhance self-confidence and self-esteem; repeating such phrases to yourself boosts self-esteem.

5. **Accentuate the positive:** There is a difference between positive thinking and focusing on the positive. Positive thinking is an expression of hope for future events. It is often characterized by setting goals, wishful thinking, and dreaming. Positive thinking can be healthy, but done to excess, it can be a form of denial. Focusing on the positive is reframing the current situation. It is an appreciation of the present moment. Acknowledge the negative. Learn from it, but don't dwell on it. Focus on the positive aspects, and build on them. A rose has both petals and thorns; which do you focus your attention on? As a personal example, try to find five positive aspects of the first problem you listed in Exercise 1 in Chapter 1.

Ultimately, we alone are responsible for the creation of our own thoughts. Shifting our thoughts from a negative stance to a positive attitude is necessary to break the cycle of perceptions that promote stressful threats.

Situations can offer both positive and negative experiences, like a rose, which has both petals and thorns. Where do you choose to place your attention?

Creativity is not a gift for the chosen few; it is a birthright for all individuals. (Left, actor/comedian Robin Williams; Right, inventor/artist Leonardo da Vinci)

Creative Problem Solving

Creativity, the mother of invention and the father of play, is talent that resides within each and every one of us. Creativity is not a gift, it is a human birthright. But like muscles that shrink with disuse, creativity must be regularly exercised to be effective. Stress is often defined as any change in our environment, and creativity has the ability to make change palatable, perhaps enjoyable. But creativity takes the right attitude and a workable strategy. Creativity is now thought to be one of the most important stress management tools at the worksite, and for this reason, seminars in creativity are being taught in corporations across the country. If you fear that your creative abilities have slipped into hibernation, here is a refresher course in the basics of creativity.

The Creative Process   In simple terms, the creative process has two parts, *primary* and *secondary* creativity, similar to what are referred to as right and left brain functions, respectively. Primary creativity is where ideas originate. It is the playground of the mind, where ideas are generated and hatched. Secondary creativity becomes the strategic plan to implement the ideas brought in from the mind's playground. Secondary creativity is like the mind's workshop, a place to saw, chisel, glue, hammer, and polish ideas together for functional use.

In his book *A Kick in the Seat of the Pants*, creativity consultant Roger von Oech elaborates even fur-

ther by describing the creative process as being a combination of four phases: the *Explorer*, the *Artist*, the *Judge*, and the *Warrior*. The Explorer and the Artist serve in the capacity of primary creativity, and the Judge and the Warrior serve in the roles of secondary creativity. In the creative process, the objective is to let each player do its job without interference from the other three. The goal of creative processing is to sharpen the skills of all four team players so that one or two aspects don't overpower the others (that would stifle the entire creative process). Beginning with the Explorer, let us take a closer look at the various stages of the creative process.

- **The Explorer:** The Explorer searches for raw materials with which to create ideas. The most important equipment the Explorer needs is an open mind: a container in which to put the raw materials. Negative thoughts close a mind water-tight. An open mind employs several attitudes to act as a fertilizer for the mind. Among these are curiosity, optimism, and enthusiasm. To get new ideas, the Explorer must explore new territories by going outside the normal bounds and comfort zone of everyday life—for example, subscribing to a different type of magazine, visiting a museum, or going to a musical.
- **The Artist:** In the role of the Artist, the raw materials (ideas) are cultivated, manipulated, and sometimes incubated until they are molded into functional use. If the Explorer asks "Where?", then

People who say they are not creative are only limited by their own beliefs and perceptions.

the Artist asks "How and What?" In the role of the artist, you play with ideas and begin to turn them into real possibilities.

- **The Judge:** In the stage of judgment, a decision of thumbs up or thumbs down is made for each idea, with the good ideas becoming a reality. The role of the Judge is crucial, for the Judge can destroy good ideas as easily as it can make good ideas really happen. Critical thoughts and overanalysis, used at the wrong time, can dominate and destroy the other stages, resulting in a waste of both time and resources. That's why in the North American culture, the Judge (a left brain skill) is often criticized as the strongest player in the creative team.

- **The Warrior:** The Warrior runs the anchor leg on the creative relay team. The role of the Warrior, in tandem with the Judge, is to take the creative idea "to the streets." Like a quarterback, the Warrior creates an action plan, a winning game plan. There is a saying on Wall Street that "to know and not to do is not to know." Warrior skills require good organization and administrative abilities.

Creative Roadblocks   There are many reasons why the creative process gets ignored. Obstacles to creativity begin with negative attitudes perpetuating the myth that only a chosen few are truly gifted. This attitude eventually promotes a sense of creative laziness.

Some popular attitudes that inhibit the creative process, as noted by von Oech, include the following:

1. I'm not creative: Creativity isn't a perception; it is a process. When it is thought of as a perception, it can be very stifling. Everyone is creative. It just takes some effort. What separates people like Picasso, Alice Walker, and Walt Disney from those who say they are not creative? The main difference is the belief these people have in themselves that they are creative. See yourself as an untapped wellspring of creativity, and then begin to use it.

2. There is only one right answer: The typical attitude in the North American culture is that there is only one right answer to every problem. Once the apparent answer is found, everyone stops looking. In the germination phase of the creative process, there are many real possibilities. If you are searching for one right answer, you will surely stop once you have found it. In trying to solve work-related problems, nothing could be more dangerous.

3. Don't be foolish: We are afraid to say or do anything out of the ordinary for fear that we will look foolish in public. So we constantly keep our guard up. Guarded behavior promotes conformity, which in turn breeds staleness. In the creative process, this mentality can lead to a concept called *group think,* in which everyone conforms and goes along with the crowd. In the business world, group think is considered dangerous because it stifles creativity. Sometimes we need to give ourselves permission to be foolish. A giddy outlook gives us a new perspective on a situation. Playing the fool can augment the role of the Judge to determine the worthiness of ideas. Being foolish can also mean

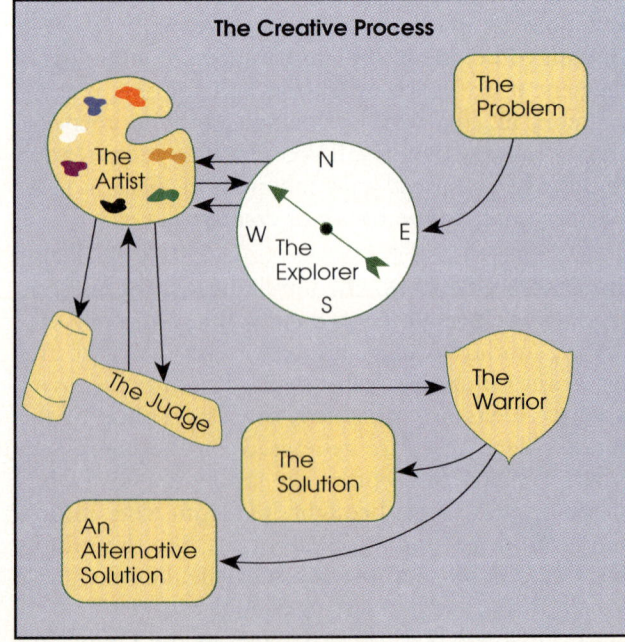

Creativity is a nonlinear process.

"Nothing is more dangerous than an idea, when it's the only one we have."
—Emile Chartier

"Every act of creation is first an act of destruction."
—Picasso

"Afflict the Comfortable, Comfort the Afflicted."
—Carl Ally

"The best way to get a good idea is to get a lot of ideas."
—Linus Pauling

"If you only have a hammer, you'll see every problem as a nail."
—Abraham Maslow

"A ship in port is safe, but that's not what ships are built for."
—Grace Hopper

"If you do not ask "why this?" often enough, somebody will ask, "why you?"
—Tom Hirshfield

"Slaying Sacred Cows makes great steaks!"
—Dick Nicolosi

"To know and not to do, is not to know."
—Wall Street slogan

"The only person who likes change is a wet baby."
—Roger von Oech

"If you are not failing every now and again, it's a sign that you're not trying anything very innovative."
—Woody Allen

"No one ever achieved greatness by playing it safe."
—Harry Gray

"The way to success is to double your rate of failure."
—Thomas J. Watson (IBM founder)

"Discovery consists of looking at the same thing as everyone else and thinking something different."
—Albert Gyorgryi

Source: *A Whack on the Side of the Head,* by Roger von Oech. Warner Books, New York, 1983.

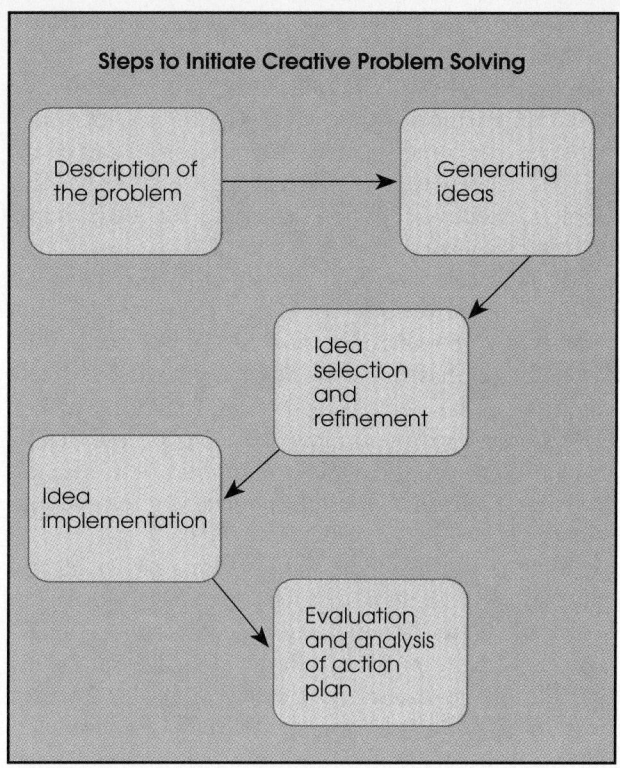

Steps to Initiate Creative Problem Solving

The map of creative problem solving.

propriate course of action. Mistakes can teach us how *not to do* something. Early in the creative process, mistakes are necessary. Each mistake clears a path to a more viable answer. The fear of failure can immobilize the creative process. In the words of Thomas J. Watson, founder of IBM, "The way to success is to double your rate of failure."

From Creativity to Creative Problem Solving As a coping technique, creativity is perhaps *the* most valuable weapon to use in your personal battle against stress. Not only does creativity boost self-esteem, but the more options you have for solving a problem, the better your chances to reduce stress. At first glance, creative problem solving might appear to be a linear process: getting from point A to point B. In reality, the problem-solving process, much like the problem itself, is more roundabout.

Steps to Initiate Creative Problem Solving The following is a five-point strategy for using the creative process to untangle personal and professional problems.

1. **Description of the problem:** Before you can attack a problem successfully, you have to understand it. State the problem objectively. Define it. Next, analyze the problem. Dissect it. Look at its components. What are its strengths and weaknesses? What is the face value, and what is the bottom line?

using your sense of humor, which in itself is a great coping technique.

4. **Avoid mistakes:** There are times when making a mistake is not a good idea. It may cost you your job, marriage, or life. Then again, there are times when making a mistake can result in the most ap-

2. Generating ideas: Generating ideas is fun. It's also challenging. Ideas can come from any available resource, internal or external. Books, people, movies, museums, memory—you name it! This is where the Explorer role comes in. The more ideas you can come up with, the better your chances are to solve the problem effectively. When searching for ideas, leave the mind's censorship role behind.

3. Idea selection and refinement: Not all ideas will be good or usable. Once your ideas are laid out on a table, one or two are going to jump out at you. Rank (Judge) these ideas by degree of feasibility (plan A, plan B, plan C, etc.). Once you have made your selection, begin to manipulate the idea to best fit the problem. This might mean streamlining the idea or changing it a little by making some alterations to suit your direct needs.

4. Idea implementation: Implementation means formulating a game plan to try the idea out, to see whether it floats or sinks. This means asking, "How can this idea be put into effect to resolve the problem?" Implementation involves a strategy and an element of risk. In addition to bravery (risk taking), implementation requires faith. An idea without faith is like a car without wheels.

5. Evaluation and analysis of action plan: A good inventor watches to see how well his or her invention works. And when the series of tests is through, either a bottle of champagne is opened or there's a return trip to the drawing board. The final lesson that a problem has to offer is *if* and *how well* it was resolved.

We all have the skills to be creative. The question is whether or not we choose to use them. In an effort to explain the importance of creativity, psychologist Abraham Maslow once said, "If you only have a hammer, you'll see every problem as a nail." He was con-

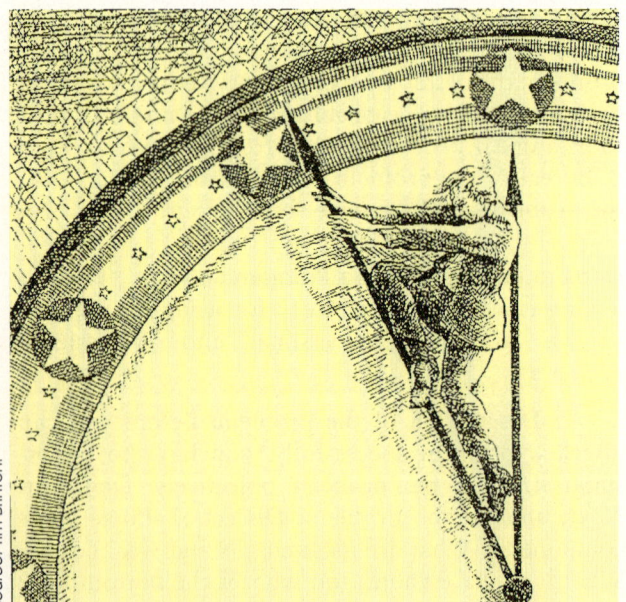

Putting in extra time "after hours" does not always indicate increased productivity. It may, in fact, be a sign of time wasted during the working day.

vinced that creativity is the necessary skill to deal with the stress of change. As a coping technique, there really is no choice if you want to deal effectively with stress. Creative problem-solving skills are life skills, skills that you need to not only survive but thrive in the chaos of change. These skills, once refined, can and should be used repeatedly as the foundation of every strategy used to confront and resolve stress.

Time Management

Time as a measurable quantity is an artificial concept. Seconds, hours, days, months, and years are creations of the human mind. From calendars to digital watches, the quantification of time has been an effort to make order out of chaos. Yet today, rather than serving us, time has become the master, and we its servants. Time management is a relatively new concept in both personal and professional development. Time management can be defined as the ability to prioritize, schedule, and execute personal responsibilities to personal satisfaction. Corporations spend great amounts of time and money to train their employees to manage time more efficiently for greater work productivity. These same skills can be used in other aspects of your life as well. The following are some lessons in time management.

Roadblocks to Effective Time Management Before you can begin to use these strategies to make better use of your time, it is best to become aware of any habits you have that waste time. Six distinct behaviors have been noted as "time robbers" because they steal valuable time, rather than promote effective time usage. As you read these, see whether any apply to you.

- **Type A personality:** Type A people display behaviors that include a rush to meet deadlines, lack of planning, poor organizational skills, and trying to

Procrastination can come in many forms, including talking to co-workers, cleaning one's desk, or playing computer games instead of doing one's job.

accomplish everything at once, getting little done in the process.

- **Workaholic:** Workaholism is described as a behavior in which a person spends excessive, but not necessarily productive, time at work, usually to compensate for low self-esteem. In many cases, workaholics bring their work home with them, too.

- **Time juggler:** A time juggler tends to overlook his or her appointments, committing to be at more than one place at a time (e.g., a staff meeting and a child's school meeting). These people end up making brief appearances at both events or skipping one altogether. In either case, quantity and quality of time are lacking.

- **Procrastinator:** Procrastination is a diversion tactic to avoid responsibilities. Four factors are associated with procrastination: laziness, apathy, the fear of failure, and the need for instant gratification. Procrastinators end up rushing to do a job that they really had plenty of time to do. In most cases, work takes priority over home responsibilities, and the family suffers.

- **Perfectionist:** A perfectionist is someone who shows obsessive, even compulsive behavior by attempting to complete every task and responsibility to perfection. He or she tends to get caught up in small details, at the cost of finishing the job by its deadline.

- **Lifestyle behavior trap:** People who fall into the lifestyle behavior trap are individuals who have a hard, if not impossible, time saying "no." This behavior leaves no time for themselves. Feelings of being taken advantage are common with this behavior.

Steps to Initiate Time Management Techniques

Once again, the definition of time management is the ability to prioritize, schedule, and execute personal responsibilities to personal satisfaction. This suggests three types of effective time management skills: prioritization, scheduling, and execution of personal responsibilities.

1. **Prioritization:** Prioritization means ranking responsibilities and tasks in their order of importance. Before this can be done, however, a list of all current responsibilities must be made. Three methods are advocated in the prioritization process: *The ABC Rank Order Method*, the *Pareto Principle*, and the *Important Versus Urgent Method*.
   a. *The ABC Rank Order Method* involves assigning the letter A, B, or C to each responsibility in the following fashion: An A-rating is given to the highest-priority activities, labeled "MUST DO IMMEDIATELY"; a B-rating is assigned to less important activities (anything that is not an A or C rating), labeled "SHOULD DO SOON"; and a C-rating is given to low-priority tasks or things that you would like to do, earmarked "CAN WAIT TO DO."
   b. *The Pareto Principle* states that 80% of the rewards or satisfaction comes from only 20% of the tasks that we do. Also referred to as the 80/20 Rule, this principle suggests that you should focus on the two most significant tasks that will maximize the benefits of your invested time.
   c. Sometimes it is difficult to assign priorities to responsibilities when they all seem important. In this case, try a method of prioritization in which responsibilities are grouped by both importance and urgency. To use the *Important Versus Urgent Method*, divide your daily or weekly responsibilities into the four boxes shown in Exercise 3C.

2. **Scheduling:** Scheduling is "time allocation" for prioritized responsibilities, or the skill of matching a specific task or responsibility with a designated time period in which to accomplish it. Time management experts advocate the three C's method and the three P's method for scheduling. The three C's method includes *Clocks*, tasks performed at a specific time in the day; *Calendars*, weekly, monthly, and even yearly forecasts of future goals and responsibilities; and *Completion Times*, designated dates and times to complete goals and responsibilities. The Three P's method includes *Planning*, implementing the schedule of tasks; *Priorities*, making a regular check on the relative importance of tasks; and, perhaps most important, *Pacing*, the rate at which tasks are performed. Please remember, it is paramount to be flexible in your scheduling (e.g., make time for interruptions), or these time management techniques will *cause* stress rather than reduce it.

3. **Execution:** Execution can best be described as putting the established schedule into action. Peo-

ple need more than a leap of faith to go from prioritization and scheduling to completion and closure of required responsibilities. A prioritized schedule is like a blueprint or a cooking recipe. Here are some tips to improve the execution of specific tasks.

a. *Break large projects down into smaller tasks.* Assign a deadline for each section of the project (the divide and conquer method of business).

b. *Work on one section or task at a time.* Also, work on that task until it is complete. Experts indicate that it is better to have one or two completed tasks than a handful of unfinished jobs.

c. *Reward your accomplishments.* Designate a goal and a reward to motivate yourself for the completion of the task. *Caution:* Avoid the immediate gratification syndrome. In other words, the reward comes *after* the satisfactory completion of each job, not before.

Some Additional Time Management Ideas The following are some additional ideas that don't fit into any specific category but nevertheless are helpful hints for managing your time effectively:

1. **Delegate:** When appropriate, learn to delegate responsibilities. Delegation involves trusting yourself to give up control as well as trusting the people to whom you delegate responsibilities. Be careful not delegate responsibilities for which the time to explain the task would take longer than the time to complete the task itself. When you delegate responsibilities, explain instructions clearly, assign a completion time or date for each task,

Remember that many situations that seem like interruptions of the job you are doing are, in fact, part of your job. Allocate some time each hour for interruptions such as phone calls or impromptu office visits.

and follow up once the task is completed. Give positive feedback when appropriate.

2. **Schedule interruptions:** Learn to be flexible with you work schedule. Feelings of frustration, impatience, and anger can result when you feel violated by interruptions. However, if you allow for a small number of interruptions in your day, the feelings of anger and hurriedness can be minimized. Experts suggest that interruptions can actually be scheduled into your daily activities by allotting 7–10 minutes per hour for interruptions. Conversely, interruptions can also be blocked out of crucial time periods when you just cannot be interrupted. Strategies for doing this may include taking the phone off the hook, closing the office door, or leaving the worksite (if possible) for periods of time when distractions are unavoidable.

3. **Schedule personal time in each day:** Experts agree that a day filled to the brim with career and family responsibilities, leaving no time for yourself, results in burnout. This can be the first step to disease and illness. Your health should be a top priority! Quality alone time allocated for exercise and/or meditation is crucial to the quality of your work performance.

4. **Keep an idea book:** An idea book, like a journal, is a place to record various ideas that call for your attention at the most awkward moments. An idea book, like a second brain, can become a receptacle for a multitude of important thoughts. Once you have written them down, you can refer back to them at any time. An idea book can include "TO DO" lists, business strategies, dream lists, names and phone numbers, or any idea that you don't want to forget.

5. **Edit your life:** Make a list of those factors that are essential to the core to your life (e.g., family) and those factors that are on the edge, people or obligations that drain your energy and can be edited out. Make it a point to cut these loose by editing them from your daily routine and personal space.

6. **Network:** Tracking down resources to accomplish tasks can be a waste of time if it takes too long to locate them. People are resources, and your connections to them are important. Networking is creating solid connections between yourself and these acquaintances. In reviewing your network of people resources, learn who can help you in times of need and who cannot be counted on.

7. **Sharpen your organizational skills:** The following are some tips to help sharpen your organizational skills:

a. *A place for everything and everything in its place:* Precious time can be saved by designating a place for bills, memos, assignments, budget sheets, and the like and keeping these items where they belong.

b. *Access your resources:* Learn *what* resources are available to complete what you need to get done, and learn *where* these resources are and *when* you can use them.

c. *Buy one master calendar or daily planner:* Write down all your project deadlines in one calendar to get a global picture of the events in your life. Learn to look at the entire week and month at a glance to get a wide perspective, then zoom in and focus on the immediate needs.

d. *Learn to make outlines:* Outline your agendas for all meetings, projects, proposals, and presentations so that you are ready.

e. *Handle it once:* Studies show that when mail is opened and stacked to be answered, the more times that it is opened and viewed, the longer it will take to get done. Handle it once and be done with it.

8. **Learn to recognize your physical and mental limitations:** Learn *how* to say "no" to people who plead for time you don't have (e.g., "I'm sorry, but I simply don't have time."). Be gentle but firm! Learn *when* to say "no" to people who plead for time you don't have.

Time management is not a control of time. Rather, it is your ability to use your time more efficiently when personal responsibilities accumulate. These time management techniques themselves can be stressful if careful planning and flexibility are not budgeted into the process.

Interpersonal Coping Skills

Communication Skills

In the words of John Donne, "No man is an island, entire of itself; every man is a piece of the continent, a part of the main." Our lives are filled with interpersonal interaction, especially on the job. Experts indicate that the average person spends approximately three quarters of his or her waking day communicating with other people. Different people's communication styles and the many possible meanings of even the most common words leave much room for misinterpretation, misunderstanding, and stress. This occurs particularly during communication between supervisors and employees. To help minimize and resolve stressful misunderstandings in the work environment, good communication skills are extremely important. To be a good communicator, you must not only express your thoughts and feelings in understandable words, but also *listen* to perceive and understand information as it is intended.

Communication skills are considered so important in the business world that workshops and seminars are given regularly on this topic; poor

The average person spends approximately three quarters of his or her waking day communicating with others, leaving much room for misunderstanding and frustration.

communication skills are simply not cost effective. The following skills, as taught in these seminars, are based on common sense. Yet common sense and good communication skills are often compromised or forgotten under work-related pressure. By reacquainting yourself with these skills you can improve the way you communicate in the workplace to minimize job stress.

Conversation Styles   It is well documented that the sexes tend to have different communication styles, as do people from different geographic locations. This is also true of personality types. These communication styles include, but are not limited to, the dominant, interruptive, manipulative, polite, creative, sarcastic, and passive means of self-expression. When you interact with someone who has a style that is different from your own, friction can occur, and conflict can escalate. Moreover, when you are feeling stressed, your own style may become exaggerated, and this widens the gap of misunderstanding even further. Whether out of politeness, fear, or manipulation, people tend to be indirect, rather than direct with the messages they communicate. A serious problem can occur when what we really want to say is stated indirectly and then misinterpreted. The result is more misunderstanding and potential conflict. Remember that verbal communication is just one of several ways to communicate a message. Messages are also stated nonverbally, with our postures, clothes, proximity, and facial expressions. Interestingly enough, people tend to believe nonverbal messages over spoken messages when the two contradict each other.

Many words have multiple meanings and miscommunication can occur where there is the slightest degree of interpretation.

Speak with Directness A guide to interpersonal communication can be summed up in these words: Say exactly what you mean, and mean what you say. In other words, *be direct*. Implementing this rule in your conversation style, however, can be extremely difficult. One reason why confusion arises from verbal communication is that our ideas and feelings are really limited by our choice of words. And some thoughts just cannot be expressed verbally. Obviously, if you have a limited vocabulary, you will have a more difficult time expressing how you think and feel. Unfortunately, even when our vocabulary does appear to adequately describe our thoughts, we often camouflage our true feelings with words to avoid hurting the feelings of others and even ourselves. This, too, can produce stress.

Listening and Responding Skills As a rule, people hear, but they do not listen very well. Several key factors involved in listening, attending, and responding skills are the following.

1. Assume the role of a listener: Listening requires that all attention be paid to what the person you are conversing with is saying. Your mind should be clear of all thoughts that distract attention away from the speaker. Don't prepare comments, rebuttals, and opinions while you are supposed to be listening. Take your time, and wait until it is your turn to speak.

2. Maintain eye contact: Strong eye contact is considered extremely important to effective listening. Wandering eyes suggest wandering thoughts. Moreover, the lack of eye contact conveys a lack of interest in the subject or the person. Good eye contact conveys respect for the person to whom you are listening.

3. Avoid word prejudice: Some words that we use can elicit obvious emotional responses in which the listener begins to show signs of disinterest or surprise. Words such as "feminist," "gay," "Jew," or "liberal" can press buttons and set the emotional wheels spinning. Raised eyebrows, frowns, and side glances are overt signs of word prejudice. Please be careful how you use these types of words.

4. Use minimal encouragers to indicate that you are on the same wavelength as the person speaking to you: Minimal encouragers include using short word phrases such as "oh?" and "uh-huh?" or repeating key words to encourage the person to give you more detailed information about the subject being discussed. Remember, these encouragers should be used genuinely, not mechanically.

5. Paraphrase the context of what was said to ensure clarification: Paraphrasing is a more elaborate style of minimal encouragement. In addition to repeating key words, paraphrasing includes the use of personal observations to demonstrate that the intended message was understood.

6. Ask questions to improve clarity of statements: When you are not sure you understand the facts, concepts, or feelings expressed to you, ask questions to make sure that you are grasping what the person is saying. Don't be afraid to ask people to explain what they mean. But beware! Questions can sometimes put the speaker on the defensive. Use questions to clarify your understanding, not to confuse the person to whom you are listening.

7. Use empathy to reflect and share the individual's feelings: Empathy is thought to be an important attending skill. Empathy refers to the selective attention to the individual's feelings as well as thoughts. Empathy does not imply that you adopt these feelings as your own. Rather, empathy invites you to recognize these feelings in the individual to whom you are listening.

8. Provide personal feedback: Responding to comments may often require feedback from the listener. Before you offer your opinion, ask whether feedback is desired. If your viewpoint is invited, offer your comments and criticism in a constructive way, balancing positive aspects with negative perceptions. Provide details and insights toward improving the situation discussed.

9. Summarize the content of what was said: Summarization is similar to paraphrasing thoughts, yet it requires more concentration and synthesis of the person's thoughts and feelings to fully comprehend what was said. This is really important in describing details of a job.

Steps to Enhance Communication Skills   The following are additional suggestions to strengthen your communication skills and help promote conflict resolution.

1. Speak with precision and directness: Be as direct as possible with your thoughts and perceptions by selecting words that accurately express how you feel. Clearly state the intention of your message!

2. Enhance your vocabulary: A small vocabulary may actually limit your ability to express yourself, whereas a greater selection of words to choose from (especially adjectives and adverbs) will provide you with a greater flexibility to express yourself clearly.

3. Use language that is appropriate for your listening audience: The manner in which you would speak with a CEO may differ from that which you would use with a custodian. Assess what words, expressions, and gestures are most conducive to explaining what you really want to say.

4. Attack issues, not people: When trying to resolve conflicts between yourself and others, focus on the problem, not on the people who are involved. Avoid character assassinations. Attacking people tends to attract other concerns that cloud the issue and make it harder, if not impossible, to resolve. And when you are wrong, apologize.

5. Avoid putting others on the defensive: When initiating self-disclosure or a dialogue to resolve conflicts, begin your statements with the words, "I perceive that . . ." By placing the responsibility of understanding on yourself, rather than blaming others, you minimize putting others on the defensive and prolonging the conflict.

6. Avoid indirect communication: Do not ask someone else to pass on your thoughts or intentions to a third party. The most effective communication involves direct contact. Involving a third party (e.g., "please tell my assistant to bring the Johnson files") not only increases the chances for miscommunication of the intended message, it also sends nonverbal messages.

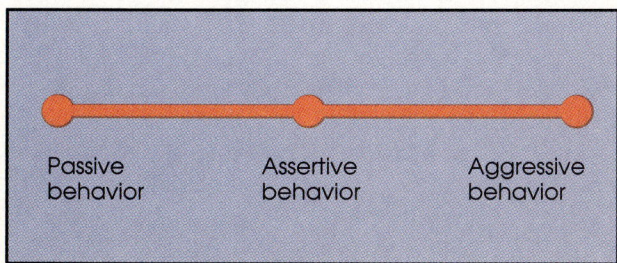

Styles of behavior.

7. Avoid information overload: Pace your conversation to allow people ample time to understand the information that you have expressed. Avoid giving people too much information at once.

8. Double-check your assumptions: Many episodes of miscommunication result from incorrect assumptions. Even if you are sure about information or ideas from another person, it is always best to validate your perceptions before you act on them. This not only saves emotional energy, in the long run, it also saves time.

9. Resolve issues when they arise: If *you* feel that there is a problem of misunderstanding, then there probably is. Avoiding issues or giving them too much time to fester allows time to validate feelings of victimization and frustration on all sides. Try to deal with issues as they surface, by talking them out with the people who are involved. Be assertive. Indicate that there is a problem if you feel that there is one.

Good communication skills are essential in any situation. Make it a habit to employ these skills regularly in your everyday interactions in the home and work environment.

Assertiveness Skills

Assertiveness   Self-assertiveness is defined as the ability to be comfortably strong-willed with our thoughts, feelings, and actions, neither inhibited nor aggressive with our actions, to the betterment of ourselves in our environments. Self-assertiveness has become the major focus of changing stress-related behaviors, particularly in communication skills. Assertiveness is one of three styles common to human behavior, positioned in between passive and aggressive behaviors. Behavior styles at either end of the spectrum can promote stress. For example, passive behavior can promote feelings of victimization, while aggressive behavior may indicate unresolved anger.

Employing Assertiveness Skills   To change a negative behavior, you must first be aware that what you are doing is undesirable and may, in fact, be stress-promoting. Once you become aware of *and* willing to change this behavior, then an alternative behavior can be adopted. From workshops on assertiveness training come several skills that we can use in our everyday behaviors to reduce potentially stressful encounters and, at the same time, build self-esteem. These include the following:

1. **Learn to say "no":** Assertiveness training teaches you to say "no" when you cannot afford to take on additional responsibilities, without feeling guilty or that you are hurting the other person's feelings. This skill teaches people that they have the right to refuse a request without harboring feelings of guilt and resentment.

2. **Learn to use "I" statements:** The use of "I" statements encourages you to claim ownership of thoughts, feelings, opinions, perceptions, and beliefs. Assertiveness training encourages you to feel comfortable employing the skills to express your feelings and opinions using "I" statements (e.g., "I feel angry about . . . " or "I perceive what you said to me to be incorrect.")

Body language can be more revealing than the spoken word; people are more likely to trust body language than verbal communication when the two differ.

3. **Use eye contact:** The lack of eye contact is perceived by others as either expressing dishonesty or discomfort about what you are saying. Eye contact is often most difficult when you express your feelings toward someone else, for fear of rejection. Assertiveness training encourages you to use eye contact while expressing your thoughts, feelings, and opinions to others. Start with a short time interval (1–2 seconds) and progress to periods of 8–10 seconds. Remember, though, that just as poor eye contact communicates lack of confidence, staring (prolonged eye contact) is perceived to be a violation of personal space and should be avoided.

4. **Use assertive body language:** How you stand and position your arms, legs, and body can either reinforce your message or detract from it. In addition to eye contact and a reassuring tone of voice, how you carry yourself (your posture and head position) unconsciously reveals how you really feel about the messages you are communicating. When you talk to someone, your posture should be straight, chin up, with your body weight equally distributed between both legs, and your center of gravity maintained directly above your feet.

5. **Practice peaceful disagreement:** When opinions and facts are voiced peacefully, so that all perspectives can be viewed in a decision-making process, then disagreement is considered healthy. This assertiveness skill allows you to become comfortable with what is called *peaceful confrontation*. Use this

Being assertive means learning how to say "No."

skill when you feel a need to express your opposing view and let your voice be heard.

6. Avoid manipulation: When asserting yourself, you may find that others, in an effort to control the situation, purposely try to block your efforts to resolve the issue at hand. Manipulation can come in the forms of intimidation, content substitution, personal attacks, or avoidance. Be careful not to allow others to derail your assertiveness with *their* style of manipulation.

7. Respond rather than react: A reaction is a reflex based on emotional thoughts. A response, on the other hand, is a thought-out strategy to a situation. Many times, we react rather than respond. We often wish we had thought before we spoke or acted on a situation. Learning to respond to a situation means taking your time to think of an appropriate response to the situation at hand and use it.

Many behaviors either trigger or continue the stress response. Change comes about through a desire to abandon old behaviors and replace them with a new, more suitable action that helps to resolve issues that you perceive to be stressful. Assertiveness skills are those behaviors that allow you to feel and express your emotions, opinions, and rights as a human being. Self-assertion is neither a passive attitude that fosters approval and subsequent resentment nor an aggressive style that intimidates others. When you find yourself being taken advantage of, ask yourself, "Was I assertive?"

Conflict Resolution

Regardless of how effective you might think your communication skills are, even with the best intentions there is abundant room for misunderstanding and conflict. Ideally, conflicts are best handled when they are resolved right away. However, not every sit-

Conflicts often arise when expectations are unmet or people feel the need to defend their opinions.

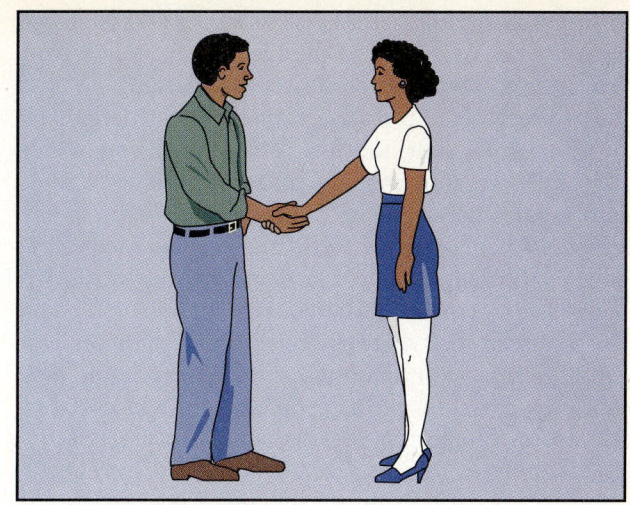

The sooner you can resolve a conflict, the better for all involved.

uation allows this opportunity (e.g., when a boss faxes you a memo at 4:50 P.M. asking you to hand in a report by 5:00 P.M., this conflict must be resolved at a later date). Usually, you need some time to organize your thoughts to effectively resolve a conflict. Regardless, the sooner you respond to a conflict, the better. The following are effective and ineffective conflict styles. Focus on the effective styles, and practice using these when a conflict situation arises at work.

Conflict Management Styles There are several management styles for dealing with conflict. Not all styles are beneficial; in fact, some may actually throw gas on the fire. Although not all situations will elicit the same response, it is important to recognize your dominant style and make changes when necessary. The following descriptions offer views of both negative and positive conflict management styles.

1. Withdrawal (negative): Withdrawal can be defined as either a physical or psychological removal from the problem. Walking out of a room, taking a detour to your office, or merely remaining silent in the midst of a conversation are examples of withdrawal or avoidance. Typically, withdrawal is regarded as an immature behavior, and thus a negative conflict management style, because a physical or verbal absence never resolves anything.

2. Surrender (negative): Like withdrawal, surrender is a type of avoidance that people use to appease co-workers, family members, peers, and close friends for fear of rejection and damaging relationships. Surrendering to the will of others by constantly giving in deflates self-esteem. This style of conflict management often generates feelings of victimization.

3. Hostile aggression (negative): Verbal aggression and underhanded tactics are often used as a form of intimidation to manipulate others. Aggressive behavior does not result in the resolution of any conflict and, in fact, often increases resentment.

4. Persuasion (positive): Persuasion is defined as an attempt to alter another person's attitude or behavior. Persuasion may include the use of reason, emotional awareness, or motivation to get a point across. When used tactfully, persuasion opens new lines of thinking, which can then be tools to resolve issues and promote mutual agreement.

5. Open dialogue (positive): Open dialogue is a verbal exchange of opinions, attitudes, facts, and perceptions shared by all the people who are involved in the problem. During the dialogue process, discussions center on the costs and benefits involved in the steps to creative problem solving. The element of compromise plays an important role in the dialogue process so that a decision is made that is agreeable to everyone. We advocate this style above all others.

Developing Support Networks

A strong social network is now considered to be a crucial factor in dealing with stress. Having good

Having a strong circle of friends tends to buffer the ill effects of stress, making your social support group an essential part of your health.

friends to count on in times of need is a true blessing and can help buffer the effects of stress.

When factors are evaluated to determine the longevity and quality of life of today's elderly, one characteristic repeatedly surfaces. No longer are proper diet, regular exercise, adequate sleep, not smoking, low blood pressure, and moderate alcohol consumption considered the sole essential qualities for living a long and healthy life. A strong network of friends has consistently been shown to be an essential factor in the "quality of life" equation. In dealing with stress, we now see that individuals who have a strong support group and feel a healthy connectedness to their family and friends show a better physical and emotional tolerance to stress than those who do not. This has been called the "*buffer theory*," which holds that close friends, in times of need, tend to buffer the ill effects of stress by helping to absorb some of the tension. This aspect of connectedness becomes very important in the work environment. In cases of disgruntled employees who take revenge on managers and co-workers, it has become apparent that these individuals, as a rule, tend to feel "disconnected" and alienated from their fellow workers. Our message to everyone in today's workforce is twofold:

1. At the worksite, reframe your attitudes and change your behaviors from a competitive to a cooperative nature. Display a greater sense of acceptance, respect, and tolerance toward co-workers despite their gender, race, management position, political persuasion, or differing characteristics.

2. Don't spread yourself too thin. Rather than trying to maintain strong friendships with many acquaintances, choose a handful of friends to be close to, both within and outside your family, to be your support group. Spend quality time to develop these relationships within your support group.

• EXERCISE 1 •
Converting Threats to Challenges

1. Describe a work-related problem you are currently facing:

2. Describe your feelings about it (e.g., anger or fear):

3. Reframe the problem so that it is now presented as a challenge rather than a threat:

4. Reframe the problem from a third perspective, also as a challenge, not a threat:

We must learn to confront our stressors.

• EXERCISE 2 •
Creating Solutions

Using this suggested format, see what you come up with for this hypothetical problem. Then, using the same format, work on a problem that you are trying to solve yourself. You might wish to refer to what you wrote down in Exercise 1.

Problem 1: Keeping Pace with Technology

Situation: Fax machines, voice mail, Express Mail, and computers seem to run your life. How can you gain a sense of control?

1. Description of the Problem:

2. Generating Ideas (Think of at least four viable possibilities):

3. Idea Selection and Refinement:

4. Idea Implementation:

5. Evaluation and Analysis of Action Plan:

• EXERCISE 3 •
Time Management Skills Worksheet
Prioritizing

A. "To Do List"

Date _____

Write down all the things you need to get done today, with no regard for order:

1.
2.
3.
4.
5.
6.
7.

B. ABC Rank Order Method of Time Management

Directions: After completing the list above, place in Column A list all the things that MUST GET DONE as soon as possible. In Column C, list all the times that you would like to do but are not essential (e.g., watching TV). In Column B, put everything else.

A Must Do	B Should Do	C Want To Do
_____	_____	_____
_____	_____	_____
_____	_____	_____

If, after doing this, you still are unsure of what tasks to do first, try organizing your list of things to do in the Important Versus Urgent Method.

C. Important Versus Urgent Method

Responsibilities

High	III a.
	      b.
	      c.
		I a.
		    b.
		    c.

	IV a.
	     b.
	 Low c.
		II a.
		     b.
		     c.

	Low	High

Urgency (vertical axis label)

Importance

Then begin to work on these tasks in the following order:

I.   a. _____
     b. _____
     c. _____

II. a. _____
     b. _____
     c. _____

III. a. _____

    b. _____

    c. _____

IV. a. _____

    b. _____

    c. _____

Scheduling

Once you have a solid idea of what needs to get done, you can make several choices about scheduling these responsibilities so that they will get done. If you have a few major projects to do, try the boxing method. If you have a zillion little things to do, try the time-mapping schedule.

Boxing

Divide your day into five parts: morning, noon hour, afternoon, dinner hour, and evening. Then write down the significant tasks, and assign to each a block of time that is most conducive to accomplishing your day's work.

1. 8:00 A.M.–12:00 noon_____

2. 12:00–1:00 P.M. _____Lunch _____(perhaps do some small errands) _____

3. 1:00–6:00 P.M. _____

4. 6:00–7:00 P.M. _____Dinner _____(exercise) _____

5. 7:00–10:00 P.M. _____

    Remember, to be effective, you will want to take small breaks during these large blocks of time.

Time Mapping

8:00 A.M._____

8:30 _____

9:00 _____

9:30 _____

10:00 _____

10:30 _____

11:00 _____

11:30 _____

12:00 noon_____

12:30 P.M. _____

1:00 _____

1:30 _____

2:00 _____

2:30 _____

3:00 _____

3:30 _____

4:00 _____

4:30 _____

5:00 _____

5:30 _____

6:00 _____

Execution

Sometimes, to get motivated to get things done, you need to outline some objectives. You might also want to reward yourself when the task is completed. These two factors are helpful in getting the job done.

Take a moment to write down some of your objectives for the day, week, or even month to get a bigger picture of what your personal strategy is. Objectives are usually big in scope and context. Goals are steps to help you accomplish your objectives. Next to each objective, think of a reward that you can give to yourself upon completion of this task. Remember, the bigger the job, the bigger the reward. In addition, remember to avoid instant gratification by seeking the reward before the task is accomplished.

Objective	Reward
1. To _____	_____
2. To _____	_____
3. To _____	_____
4. To _____	_____
5. To _____	_____
6. To _____	_____
7. To _____	_____
8. To _____	_____
9. To _____	_____
10. To _____	_____

• EXERCISE 4 •
Assertiveness Skills

The following is an exercise to increase your awareness about your own assertiveness skills. These examples are hypothetical circumstances that could produce feelings of anger, fear, and potential victimization. Write your initial response in the space provided, followed by a more assertive response if needed.

Situation: Job Performance Appraisal: A photocopy of your job performance evaluation is submitted to you, and you are angry that (a) it was completed *without* a meeting between you and your boss and (b) the poor rating is based on several inaccuracies.

Initial Reaction:

Assertive Response:

Situation: Using Assertiveness Skills: Changes in restructuring have resulted in shifts in responsibilities at the worksite. One of your favorite co-workers asks you if you can help her so she can leave early for an appointment. You are swamped with deadlines yourself.

Initial Reaction:

Assertive Response:

• EXERCISE 5 •

Identifying Your Support Network

Take a moment to make an inventory of your support network and determine what steps you can take to strengthen your ties with individuals who can provide you with support.

1. List three people at work with whom you feel comfortable enough to trust and confide in about your present work situation.

    a. _____

    b. _____

    c. _____

2. List three people, outside your family, with whom you make a regular habit of spending quality time.

    a. _____

    b. _____

    c. _____

3. Make a list of three interests or activities in which you participate outside of work and home.

    a. _____

    b. _____

    c. _____

4. Locate two groups of people in your area who share a similar interest that you could connect with once or twice a month.

    a. _____

    b. _____

5. Is there anyone on any of these lists which whom you have not been in touch lately, whom you could contact and meet with to solidify your bond of friendship?

    a. _____

    b. _____

    c. _____

4

Relaxation Techniques

Physical Relaxation Techniques • Mental Relaxation Techniques

That the birds fly overhead, this you cannot stop. That they build a nest in your hair, this you can prevent.
—Ancient Chinese proverb

We are always absorbing messages from our five senses: sight, sound, smell, taste, and touch. Information picked up through one or more of these senses is continually sent to the brain. If a message is considered to be a threat, then an alarm is sounded, and the body is prepared to move as a means of survival. It would make sense, then, that to relax from any sort of "panicked response" and return the body to a state of calmness or homeostasis, something must be done to turn down the amount of stimulation taken in by the five senses. In other words, the five senses must be *deactivated* or *reprogrammed,* if only temporarily, to give a new signal to the body to calm down. The primary purpose of relaxation techniques is to intercept the stress response, specifically in the nervous and hormonal systems. Ultimately, relaxation techniques help to prevent or minimize the physical symptoms of stress when the body works overtime to keep up with everyday worries.

Unfortunately, relaxation techniques are not a form of magic. What may work for one person to provide a calming effect may offer nothing but added frustration to others. The ability to relax is largely dependent on the individual. In addition, there is no one technique that is effective for all people in all circumstances. What we suggest is that you become familiar with several techniques so that you can pick one or two that you like to make your body more resistant to the effects of stress. Just like typing on a keyboard or hitting a golf ball, relaxation techniques are skills, and you need to practice them regularly to get the full benefits. Regardless of which technique you choose, we recommend that you practice some form of relaxation every day, for about a 20- to 30-minute period. Done regularly, these skills

will provide you with the best defense against the hazards of the stressful wear and tear on your body and promote a greater sense of well-being.

Because the mind-body connection is so strong, you might find that relaxation techniques not only create a physical calming effect, but also seem to calm the mind. For this reason, several relaxation techniques such as jogging, meditation, and listening to music help cope with stress. One common miscon-

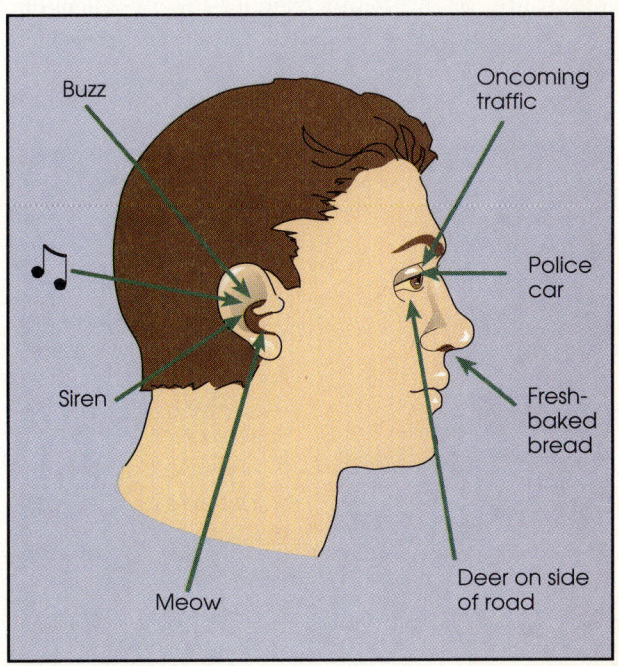

We gather information through our five senses. Relaxation techniques are used to *deactivate* the sensory organs and allow the body a chance to return to a resting state.

ception is that relaxation is the same thing as sleep. Nothing could be further from the truth. These techniques may make you sleep better, but sleeping should not be used in place of proper relaxation skills.

The origins of these relaxation techniques span many continents and cultures over several thousands of years. For example, from the Orient and Asia come the techniques of diaphragmatic breathing, yoga, meditation, massage therapy, and T'ai Chi. Several aspects of these are now combined with many Western techniques such as mental imagery, autogenic training, music therapy, and physical exercise. Once you feel confident performing these techniques, you will find that some are better suited to deal with stress immediately, while other methods are more useful at either the beginning or the end of the day. In this section, we highlight the following ways to relax: diaphragmatic breathing, progressive muscular relaxation, autogenic training, physical exercise, meditation, and mental imagery.

Physical Relaxation Techniques

Diaphragmatic Breathing

Diaphragmatic breathing is by far the easiest method of relaxation. It is easy because breathing itself is an action that we perform normally without thought or hesitation. In its simplest form, diaphragmatic breathing is slow, conscious, deep breathing. It is symbolic of a deep sigh. We often take a big breath when we are about to regroup our thoughts, gain composure, or direct our energies for a challenging task. For cultural reasons, most people are accus-

tomed to breathing with their upper chest. (Stop for a moment, and pay attention to how you breathe.) When fast asleep, without the influence of the conscious mind, everyone reverts to a more natural breathing posture, with greater stomach expansion. What makes diaphragmatic breathing different from "normal breathing" is that this method specifically involves the *conscious movement* of the lower abdomen or belly area.

The Art of Breathing   Under normal resting conditions, the average person breathes approximately fourteen to sixteen times per minute. When you become panicked, your breathing quickens and becomes more shallow, with stronger muscular contraction of the upper chest. When the upper chest expands, neural stimulation is increased, and your vital signs (heart rate, blood pressure, etc.) begin to increase. During heavy exercise, your breathing can increase to as much as sixty times per minute because your body needs more oxygen. Yet in a relaxed state, your body's metabolism is much slower, allowing for a lower, deeper breathing cycle. When you learn to modify your breathing style (with an emphasis placed on the belly), you will be able to comfortably reduce the number of breaths to as low as three to six per minute.

The practice of diaphragmatic breathing is as old as the ancient exercises of yoga and T'ai Chi. It is now a part of virtually every relaxation technique. As its own method to relax, the practice of diaphragmatic breathing focuses on just one body sensation: feeling air slowly pass through your nose or mouth down into your lungs and back via the same pathway, to the exclusion of all other stimulation from the other senses.

Steps to Begin Diaphragmatic Breathing

1. **Assume a comfortable position:** To gain the most benefit, learn this technique in a comfortable position, either in a relaxed sitting position or lying on your back with your eyes closed. To get the full effect, loosen any constrictive clothing around your neck and waist. When you first learn this technique, place your hands over your stomach and feel its rise and fall with each breath. Once you have got this down, you can do diaphragmatic breathing just about anywhere, under any circumstance. This technique can be done while driving your car in traffic, taking part in a job performance review, waiting in line at the post office, or giving a professional presentation.

2. **Concentration:** As with all relaxation techniques, diaphragmatic breathing requires your undivided attention. Concentration can be easily interrupted by both external noises (the phone ringing) and internal thoughts ("Am I doing this right?"). When possible, take steps to minimize the external

THINGS TO DO TODAY
1. inhale
2. exhale
3. inhale
4. exhale
5. inhale
6. exhale
7. inhale
8. exhale
9. inhale
10. exhale
11. inhale
12. exhale
13. inhale

Diaphragmatic breathing focuses on expanding the stomach as you inhale.

interruptions by finding a quiet place to practice. When first learning this and other techniques that require total concentration, you will notice that sometimes your mind begins to wander. This is normal. If you find that your mind becomes preoccupied with other thoughts, just allow them to fade away, and then refocus your attention on your breathing. One suggestion is to imagine these interrupting thoughts escaping through your mouth as you exhale. Another idea is to keep a piece of paper and pen beside you and write down these thoughts as they appear, just to get them out of your head.

Diaphragmatic breathing requires a conscious decision to focus your attention solely on your breathing. It helps if you imagine following the flow of air as it enters the body, proceeds to its destination in the lower portion of the lungs, and streams back out again. Sometimes a suggestion like this can help: *"Feel the air come into your nose or mouth, down into your lungs, and feel your stomach rise, then descend back down as you exhale the air, feeling it leave your lungs, throat, and nasal cavity."* Repeat each breath like this.

You can increase your concentration by focusing on the four distinct phases of each breath:

Phase I: The inspiration, taking the air into your lungs through the passage of your nose (or mouth).

Phase II: A very slight pause before exhaling the air out of your lungs.

Phase III: The exhalation, releasing the air from your lungs and through the passage it entered.

Phase IV: A very slight pause after exhalation before the next inhalation is begun. These phases really can be noticed when you exaggerate the breath-ing cycle by taking a very slow and comfortable deep breath. When you do this, try to recognize these four phases by identifying them as they occur. Remember, do not hold your breath at any one time during each phase. Rather, learn to regulate your breathing by controlling the pace of each phase in the breathing cycle. *Diaphragmatic breathing is not the same as hyperventilation.* This style is comfortably slow, deep, and relaxed. You will feel that the most relaxing phase of breathing is the third phase, the exhalation phase. In this phase, the chest and stomach areas are relaxed, causing a calming effect throughout your whole body. It requires no effort whatsoever. When focusing on your breathing, feel how *relaxed* your whole body becomes during the phase of *exhalation,* especially your chest, shoulders, and stomach region. With practice, this relaxation will spread throughout your whole body.

3. Visualization: The use of imagery with diaphragmatic breathing can be very powerful. There are many images that can be combined with this breathing technique. Exercise 1 at the end of this chapter uses an image that may help you with this technique.

Progressive Muscular Relaxation

The body's muscles respond to perceptions of threat with neural tension, a state of contraction. As a result, muscular tension is believed to be the most common symptom of stress. Although it does not send people to hospital emergency rooms like other stress-related disorders, the overall effect can be stiffness, pain, and discomfort. In extreme cases, it can cause postural abnormalities and misalignment, as well as joint instability. With repeated neural stimulation, muscle tension can appear as tension headaches, neck stiffness, lower back pain, stomach cramps, and some forms of temporomandibular joint syndrome (TMJ).

Often, muscle tension produced from thoughts in the unconscious mind can occur while we sleep. Experts note that joint stiffness, even damaged connective tissue in the jaw, neck, shoulders, and lower back, can result from muscle tension as we sleep. Knowing all this, it is easy to see why muscle tension is thought to be the most common symptom of stress. Created in the United States by Dr. Edmund Jacobson over fifty years ago, progressive muscular relaxation (PMR) is a technique specifically designed to consciously help reduce muscle tension. You do this by first becoming consciously aware of your muscle tension levels and then reducing the level of tension through *tension release.* Currently, PMR is used as a therapy to help relieve several stress-related symptoms including insomnia, hypertension, headaches, lower back pain, and TMJ. This technique, perhaps more than any other, illustrates the importance of in-

Facial stretch.

tercepting the stress response by consciously trying to decrease muscle tension.

Jacobson's original PMR technique includes the following suggestions:

1. Try to isolate the chosen muscle group during the contraction phase, leaving all remaining muscles relaxed.
2. Try to contract similar muscle groups on both sides of the body simultaneously (e.g., both forearms).
3. Focus your attention on the intensity of the contraction, sensing the amount of tension that you produce for each muscle group.
4. During the relaxation phase of each isolated muscle group, focus your awareness on how relaxed your muscles feel. Compare this sensation with how the muscle felt when it was contracted.

The best way to do PMR is to tighten and relax each muscle group in the body, one by one. The tension phase is very short, approximately 5–10 seconds. By comparison, the relaxation phase is much longer, approximately 45 seconds. Remember that only one muscle group be should be contracted at a time, leaving all other muscle groups relaxed. It might seem hard at first not to involve surrounding muscles, but this will come with practice. When you are finished with the technique, lie still on the floor or sit still in your chair for a few minutes, and pay attention to all physical sensations. Enjoy the full sense of relaxation. Then begin to focus your thoughts on your current surroundings. By feeling the different degrees of muscle contraction, you might find that you become more aware of your own muscle tension levels in the course of a day and then become able to adjust them through *tension release*.

Steps to Initiate Progressive Muscular Relaxation

1. Position: PMR can be performed in a comfortable sitting position. However, the best position to first learn and practice this method is lying com-fortably on a carpeted floor. Your arms should rest comfortably by your sides, with your palms facing upward. Loosen any tight clothing around your neck and waist. You should remove any jewelry such as wristwatches and bracelets, as well as eyeglasses or contact lenses, if you wear them.

2. Breathing: The PMR breathing technique is quite simple. Inhale as you contract the muscles, and then exhale as you release the tension. Tension release is coordinated with the release of air in the lungs, and the relaxation of the diaphragm allows for a deeper sense of total relaxation throughout the entire body.

3. Ambiance: If possible, adjust the room temperature. A cool environment may produce unwanted muscle tension and shivering. Once you are proficient in the technique, PMR may be done anywhere: sitting in traffic, standing in line, or lying in bed trying to fall asleep. We recommend that you practice this technique on a daily basis. You should feel the effects immediately.

Progressive Muscular Relaxation Suggestions Divide the contraction of each muscle group into three intensities of 5 seconds each: 100% (all out), 50% (half the strength of the initial contraction), and 5% (a slight twinge). The relaxation phase should be approximately 45 seconds in duration following each contraction. In the release phase, take a comfortably deep breath, and feel a sense of relaxation in the muscle group that was previously tensed. Try the order of muscle groups in Exercise 2 at the end of this chapter.

The advantage of PMR is its direct approach to reducing muscle tension by contracting and relaxing specific muscle groups. The relaxation effect becomes evident when you compare the state of tension with relaxation. This technique is easy to learn and practice in a variety of settings, even in stress-prone environments such as the worksite. PMR can also be used as a prevention technique in the morning or evening to help release mounting tension levels accumulated in the course of a stressful day.

There are some cautions to be noted in using this technique. Isometric muscle tension, used during the contraction phases of PMR, increases both systolic and diastolic blood pressure, even with contractions of short duration. Individuals with hypertension, ele-

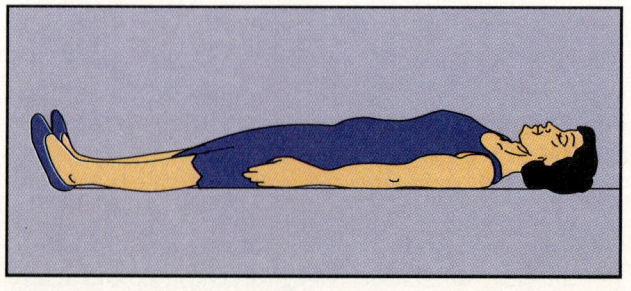

The prone position is ideal for learning PMR.

vated systolic and/or diastolic blood pressure, should not use this technique because it will certainly aggravate this condition.

Autogenic Training

The word *autogenic* means self-regulation or self-generation. It can also refer to an action that is self-produced. The term *autogenic* specifically implies that you have the ability to control various body functions such as heart rate, blood pressure, and blood flow. This is a novel concept because for centuries, specific body functions were thought to operate independently of self-directed thoughts. Research over the last two decades has proved differently. By consciously redirecting your body's responses with your own suggestions, you can help to negate the harmful effects of stress. We now know that the mind-body connection is very powerful. In fact, we can step in and take over from the automatic pilot of our nervous system whenever we want to override the stress response to nonphysical threats.

The premise of autogenic training is to learn how to "redirect" the mind with suggestions so that you can override the stress response when physical arousal is not the appropriate reaction. The primary autogenic suggestion that you give to yourself is to allow various body regions (the arms, hands, legs, and feet) to become *warm and heavy*. This sensation of warmth and heaviness, caused by a shift of blood flow (from the body's center to the desired area), acts like an internal massage, soothing and relaxing the surrounding muscles.

Steps to Initiate the Autogenic Relaxation Technique

1. Body Position: The best position for this technique is a reclining position. We suggest lying on your back on a carpeted floor or bed, with your arms by your sides, palms facing up, and legs straight with your heels resting evenly on the surface. Thin pillows or cushions may be used behind the head and knees for support, as long as the body remains comfortable with your spine straight. If circumstances do not permit you to lie down, you can perform the technique sitting straight up in a chair. While seated, keep your head aligned over your body, with your arms either on your lap or supported by the frame of the chair. You should remove watches, rings, necklaces, and chains and loosen any restrictive clothing. Perhaps most important, try not to eat a big meal before performing this technique; food in your stomach will make it less effective.

2. Concentration and awareness: In this technique, allow yourself to become open to suggestion, and adopt a passive, not defensive, frame of mind. When you first try autogenic training, you might find your mind drifting toward thoughts that seem more important. Concentration with autogenic training

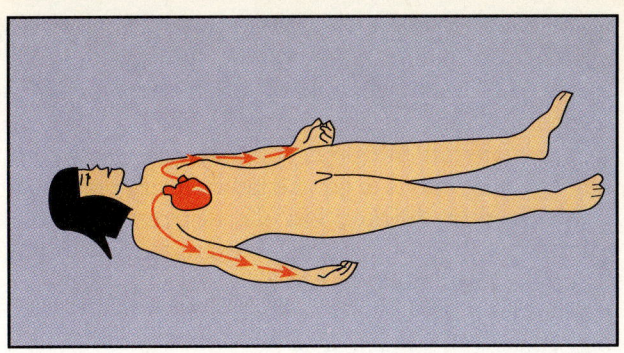

There are two suggested body positions to use in practicing this technique. The preferred method is a supine position on a comfortable floor surface. If this is not possible, then a sitting position will do fine. Once you are proficient in this technique, you can do it in any position.

concerns only the here and now, specifically the present state of your body. If at first, you find other thoughts competing for your attention, politely acknowledge them, and then focus your mind back to your body awareness. With continued practice, you will become better at the skill of concentration.

3. Phases of autogenic training: The four phases of autogenic training include a feeling of *heaviness*, a feeling of *warmth*, a *calmness of the heart*, and a *calmness of breathing*. Dedicate 3–4 minutes at each phase to repeating the instructions given in Exercise 3 at the end of this chapter until you feel the warmth, heaviness, and calmness. The entire progression of phases should take approximately 15 minutes. When you are done, remain in this position for a few moments, and try to place this feeling of relaxation into your memory bank so that you can recall it when you feel stressed.

Suggestions to Follow in Autogenic Training The principles of autogenic training can be learned quite quickly. The short-term effects are often experienced immediately. However, it might take a few weeks of practice to feel the cumulative effects. When learning and practicing autogenic training, you should practice once a day for 15 minutes so that a training effect does occur.

Originally, autogenic training was a technique to relax just the arms and hands. Today, we recommend using it to relax all body regions. The autogenic technique is as portable as the thoughts that create it. You can use it at home, at work, or anywhere. At the worksite, we suggest short periodic "autogenic breaks" in the course of a busy day as a preventive approach to the cumulative effects of the stress response.

Physical Exercise and Nutrition

For many people, physical exercise has become the most popular and effective means to reduce stress.

Quite literally, it is one of the most natural means to express the manifestation of the fight-or-flight response. Although exercise actually triggers the stress response, when you stop exercising, the body returns to a greater state of calmness than before you began. For a person who is in good condition, not only is the rate of return quicker, but the degree of physical calmness is greater than before exercise was started. It seems that the body's *natural* response, when confronted with stress, is to be active, which is why regular exercise is so beneficial.

In the past thirty years, since the recognition of coronary heart disease as North America's number one cause of death, the effects of physical exercise on the human body have been studied intensively. The overwhelming conclusion is that physical exercise is not only good, it is a virtual necessity to maintain the proper function of the body's vital organs. And just as the body requires physical calmness, it equally demands physical exercise, or certain organs won't function properly, giving credence to the expression "use it or lose it." So it becomes obvious that *there must be a balance* between physical arousal (activity) and physical calmness (rest) to achieve optimal wellness.

The primary reason why physical exercise serves as an effective relaxation technique is that stress hormones released for metabolism in the fight-or-flight response are used for their intended metabolic purpose. It seems that physical exercise actually builds an immunity to stress that strengthens the body's vital organs. Exercise physiologists have observed many positive adaptations to the cardiovascular, musculoskeletal, and immune systems when people exercise regularly. The body, it seems, can adapt to the good stress of exercise as well as the bad stress of emotional turmoil.

Types of Physical Exercise   Although there are many examples of exercise, including swimming,

Regular exercise has become one of the most popular means to reduce physical stress.

weight lifting, and golf, all physical activity falls into two categories:

1. Anaerobic exercise: Anaerobic exercise involves intense bursts of energy for short amounts of time. Weight lifting, sprints, and some calisthenics are the most common examples of this type of activity. Anaerobic exercise specifically employs muscular strength and power.

2. Aerobic exercise: Aerobic exercise or cardiovascular endurance activities are described as "rhythmic" or "continuous" in nature. Aerobic work involves moderate intensity but for an extended period of time. Intensity is typically measured by heart rate (beats per minute). Running, swimming, cycling, cross-country skiing, rhythmic dancing, and walking are great examples of aerobic activity.

Volumes of research support the idea that aerobic exercise helps to reduce the risk of heart disease

Types of exercises vary by the specific energy system used. Short bursts of activity (weight training) are considered anaerobic, whereas prolonged rhythmical exercises (swimming, walking, or jogging) are considered aerobic in nature.

Calories Burned Through Physical Activity

Swimming	Jogging	Golf	Racquetball	Aerobic Dance
249 calories	400 calories	129 calories	348 calories	201 calories

The caloric equivalent (calories burned) of swimming (crawl), jogging, golf, racquetball, and aerobic dance during a 30-minute period for a person weighing approximately 143 pounds.

Source: Seaward, Brian Luke, *Managing Stress: Principles and Strategies for Health and Wellbeing.* Jones and Bartlett, Boston, MA, 1994.

by modifying several coronary risk factors. These include:

1. A reduction of elevated blood pressure
2. A reduction of cholesterol, specifically low-density lipoproteins (LDLs)
3. Significant decreases in percent body fat
4. Increased physical activity
5. Decreased physical arousal due to stress

The Physiological Effects of Physical Exercise

First, we know that a single aerobic workout "burns off" stress hormones. These are used for their intended metabolic function, rather than lingering in the body and ruining vital organs. Therefore, exercise counters the effects of daily stressors. Second, the conditioning of aerobic exercise prepares the body for stressful situations by *not releasing* large amounts of stress hormones when feelings of anger or fear surface. In effect, exercise training tends to neutralize the physical arousal to nonphysical threats. Third, the long-term effects of exercise produced after six to eight weeks of training appear to strengthen the body's vital organs. Exercise conditioning isn't a cure for diseases and illness, nor is it the "fountain of youth." However, athletic conditioning does appear to add to both the quality and the quantity of life.

Theories of Athletic Conditioning

Numerous studies have been conducted to determine the minimal amount of exercise needed to maintain the benefits gained through physical labor. From this, we have found that four key ingredients are necessary to reap the beneficial effects of exercise. They include the following.

1. Intensity: Intensity refers the challenge (stress) placed on the body in response to the activity. It is often expressed as your target heart rate or target zone: the range of heartbeats during rhythmic exercise calculated to be in the range of 60–80% of maximal intensity. (See Exercise 4 at the end of this chapter.)

2. Frequency: Frequency refers to the number of exercise sessions in which you participate in a week. Three sessions per week is the suggested frequency needed to maintain your level of fitness.

3. Duration: Duration is the number of minutes per session. The suggested duration is a minimum of 20–30 minutes per exercise session at your target heart rate. A duration of less than 10 minutes does not guarantee the full benefits of endurance exercise.

4. Mode of exercise: The mode of exercise is the specific type of activity that is chosen to challenge your body. For example, walking, running, and swimming are considered to adequately challenge the cardiovascular system and are considered aerobic work, whereas weight training uses the anaerobic energy system.

Phases of a Workout

Just as there are guidelines to achieve the benefits of exercise, there is also a formula to follow to ensure a safe workout each time you exercise. These include (1) a proper warm-up, (2) the stimulus or conditioning period, and (3) a cool-down.

1. Warm-up period: The purpose of the warm-up is to slowly increase heart rate, allowing adequate time for the working muscles to become saturated in oxygen-rich blood. To initiate the warm-up period properly, we encourage you to do any activity such as walking, slow jogging, or calisthenics at a low intensity. Once your body is warmed up, you can stretch

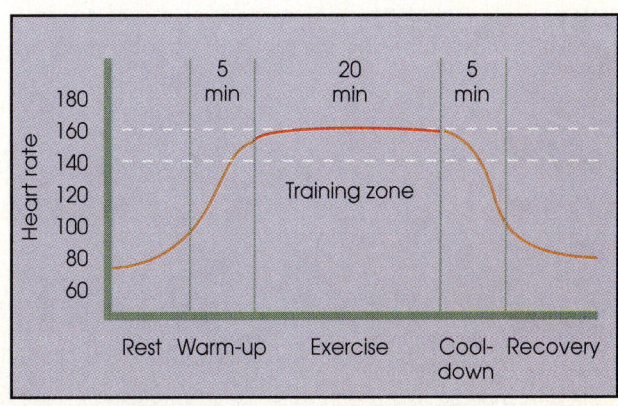

Of the three phases of a workout—warm-up, stimulus, and cool-down—the stimulus phase is when your target heart rate should remain elevated. The more efficient your cardiovascular system, the sooner your heart rate will return to a normal resting level.

A cool-down consists of decreasing your pace of activity to allow the flow of blood to return to a resting state, followed by stretching.

your muscles. Stretching before breaking into a sweat may lead to tendon or ligament damage.

2. Stimulus period: The stimulus period is the real "meat" of the workout. This is the actual period when the body's organs (e.g., heart, lungs, and muscles) are conditioned. The stimulus period should be a minimum of 20 minutes, regardless of which energy system (aerobic or anaerobic) is used. As you continue past the first eight weeks of training, you might wish to add to the duration of this workout period.

3. Cool-down period: The purpose of the cool-down period is to decrease the signs and symptoms of the stress response: heart rate, blood pressure, breathing rate, and so on. The cool-down phase, a 5- to 10-minute period, should include a decreased intensity of activity (e.g., from running to jogging to walking) followed by a few moments to stretch the muscles that were used in the activity.

Steps to Initiate a Fitness Training Program While physical exercise is now praised as one of the best ways to stay healthy, it also poses a threat to your health if it is not done correctly. The following are some suggestions regarding cardiovascular (aerobic) fitness to help avoid injury and burnout and guide you though this transition period.

1. **Set some realistic personal fitness goals for yourself.**
2. **Start cautiously and progress moderately with your program.** (If you are over thirty-five years of age, you should get a physician's approval.)
3. **Pick an activity that you really enjoy.**
4. **Select a time of day to exercise.**
5. **Exercise in the right clothes and equipment.**
6. **Initiate or join an exercise support group to stay motivated.**
7. **Try to prevent athletic injuries and properly treat any that occur.**

The Nutrition and Stress Relationship Nutrition also plays a very important role in decreasing stress in your life. There are several substances that, when eaten, tend to mimic or trigger the stress response. Likewise, stress can deplete your body of the necessary nutrients, vitamins, and minerals. Here are some examples.

1. **Sugar:** Excess amounts of simple sugars (found in soda, candy, etc.) tend to deplete vitamin stores, particularly the B-complex vitamins (niacin, thiamine, riboflavin, and B-12). When the B-complex vitamins are depleted, you might experience fatigue, anxiety, and irritability. In addition, eating large amounts of simple sugars can cause big fluctuations in your blood glucose levels, resulting in pronounced fatigue, headaches, and general irritability.

2. **Caffeine:** Food sources with caffeine trigger the stress response, specifically an increased heart rate. The result is a heightened state of alertness that makes the individual more susceptible to perceived stress. Caffeine can be found in many foods, including chocolate, coffee, tea, and several beverages.

3. **Salt:** High sodium intake from salt is associated with high blood pressure because sodium acts to increase water retention. As water volume increases

National Safety Council

**FIRST
AID
INSTITUTE**

1. ☐☐☐☐☐☐☐☐☐☐☐☐☐☐☐☐☐☐☐☐☐☐☐
   LAST NAME

2. ☐☐☐☐☐☐☐☐☐☐☐☐☐☐☐☐☐☐☐☐
   FIRST NAME

3. ☐
   MIDDLE
   INITIAL

4. ☐☐☐☐☐☐☐☐☐☐☐☐☐☐☐☐☐☐☐☐☐☐☐☐
   MAILING ADDRESS

5. ☐☐☐☐☐☐☐☐☐☐☐☐☐☐☐☐☐☐☐☐☐
   CITY

6. ☐☐
   STATE

7. ☐☐☐☐☐ – ☐☐☐☐
   ZIP CODE

MY NAME IS _____

COURSE/INSTRUCTOR EVALUATION
STRESS MANAGEMENT

Course Completion Date _____

Instructor _____

City/State _____

How did you learn about this course?

_____

How many hours did you spend on the
course? _____

How many students were in the
class? _____

How would you rate the book? _____

_____

_____

How would you rate the instructor's materials
(videos, slides, etc.)? _____

_____

How would you rate your instructor?

_____

_____

How would you improve this course?

_____

_____

_____

National Safety Council

Please describe your previous stress management training, if any: _____
_____
_____
_____
_____
_____
_____
_____
_____
_____

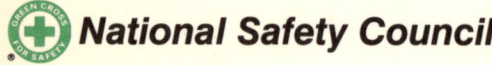 **National Safety Council**

Postage
Necessary

FAI EVALUATION

 **National Safety Council**
1121 Spring Lake Drive
Itasca, Illinois 60143-3201

A noncompetitive workout with a group of friends serves as a great motivation factor to make physical exercise a regular lifelong habit.

in a closed system, blood pressure increases. If this condition persists, it may contribute to hypertension.

4. Vitamin and mineral deficiency: Chronic stress can cause a depletion of water-soluble vitamins (B and C) that are necessary for energy metabolism. Stress can also deplete calcium stores in the body and prevent the absorption of calcium in bone tissue.

Recommendations for Healthful Eating Habits   We would like to recommend a few simple changes to your diet that can help to minimize the body's arousal to stress and enhance optimal well-being. They include the following.

1. **Eat a well-balanced diet, containing the proper amounts of carbohydrates, fats, and proteins.**
2. **Eat a good breakfast, and space meals evenly throughout the day.**
3. **Avoid or minimize the consumption of caffeine, sugar, and salt.**
4. **Eat a diet that provides adequate levels of the vitamins and minerals that are depleted by stress.**

There is no doubt about it. The body needs regular exercise. When you are tired and feel that you don't have the time, that is when you need exercise the most. Your body also needs good fuel to burn. To get the best benefits of habitual physical exercise, you need the right intensity, frequency, and duration as well as the best mode of exercise. Make it a point to

get some exercise, even if it is just going for a 20-minute walk every day.

Mental Relaxation Techniques

Meditation

Meditation is best described as an increased concentration and awareness, a process to clear the mind and *live in the present moment*. The practice of meditation is the oldest recognized relaxation technique known to all civilizations. So accepted are several components of meditation that they have been adopted into virtually every relaxation technique known and practiced.

Many studies have been done on the benefits of meditation. Research findings reveal that people who meditate regularly show fewer signs of anxiety; decreased smoking; decreased alcohol and recreational drug use; a greater sense of self-esteem, self-confidence, and self-reliance; and the ability to sleep more soundly than people who don't meditate. Today, therapists commonly use the technique of meditation as a way to promote psychological well-being. Because meditation has proven to be so effective in lowering resting heart rate, blood pressure, muscle tension, and other metabolic functions, the American Heart Association now advocates this technique as a way to help prevent coronary heart disease.

Meditation: Calming the Mind   Under stress, your mind can become overwhelmed with distractions. A closer look shows us that the mind juggles many thoughts, produced both internally (memories, feelings) and externally (conversations, traffic, radio broadcasts, etc.), all of which compete for attention. As these thoughts accumulate, our minds get cluttered, and we experience *sensory overload*. You have probably felt this at the end of a long day of

Prolonged stress can deplete vitamin stores in the body. The best source of vitamins and minerals comes from natural unprocessed food.

Typical American Diet		U.S. Government Recommended Daily Allowances	
Carbohydrates:	30–40%	Carbohydrates:	55–70%
Fats:	40–50%	Fats:	20–30%
Proteins:	20–30%	Proteins:	15–20%

Source: Seaward, Brian Luke, *Managing Stress: Principles and Strategies for Health and Wellbeing.* Jones and Bartlett, Boston, MA, 1994.

work. Sensory overload is like a blackboard filled to capacity with notes, scribbles, and information that is quite difficult to organize and understand. To carry this metaphor one step further, meditation is like an eraser that cleans the mind's blackboard. When our minds are overloaded and cluttered with information, our attention span is shortened. A cluttered mind becomes a stressed mind. Meditation is a tool to *unclutter the mind* and bring about mental tranquillity. When your mind becomes clear of cluttered thoughts, you become more receptive to intuitive insight, new perspectives, and new ways of dealing with your unresolved problems. This is the primary purpose of meditation: increased concentration, which promotes self-awareness. So as the ancient Chinese proverb says, "When the student is ready, the teacher will come."

Meditation itself is not a religion. Rather it is a practice of becoming quiet and taming thoughts and perceptions that promote sensations of stress.

Types of Meditation From the seeds of Eastern philosophy grew two distinct branches of meditation: *exclusive* (restrictive meditation) and *inclusive* (opening-up meditation). Although they vary in style and format, the result is the same: a cleansing of the mind that that leads to a sensation that can best be described as "inner peace."

Exclusive Meditation: Exclusive meditation (also known as *concentration meditation*) asks that you restrict your attention to a single thought. This single thought becomes a device to rid all other thoughts from your mind. A single thought is like a gentle wind that blows the clouds away, leaving a clear blue sky. The power of this single thought is its repetition, which continually breaks the surface of attention, like ocean waves, to the exclusion of all other thoughts. The restrictive meditation process asks that you close your mind to external sensations and all outside stimulation and then direct the focus of your thoughts inward. In most cases, exclusive meditation is practiced with the eyes closed to prevent visual distractions.

The five methods that can help to bring your attention to a single focused thought are:

1. Mental repetition: Mental repetition is a thought that is repeated over and over and over again. This mental repetition is most commonly done through the use of a *mantra*, specifically a one-syllable word (e.g., "OM," "one," "peace," or "love") that is repeated silently with the exhalation of each breath.

2. Visual concentration: Visual concentration involves staring at an object or image. Common "visual mantras" include a candle flame, a flower, a sea shell, a beautiful picturesque scene, or a mandala.

3. Repeated sounds: Examples of repetitive sounds are a beating drum, chimes, Tibetan bells, Gregorian chants, the rush of a waterfall, the sound of gentle ocean waves, rolling thunder, and some types of instrumental music.

4. Physical repetitive motion: Repetitive motions such as breathing and some forms of rhythmic aerobic exercise (e.g., running, swimming, or walking) are believed to produced a meditative state (the "runner's high").

5. Repeated tactile motion: Holding and manipulating a small object such as a tumble stone, a sea

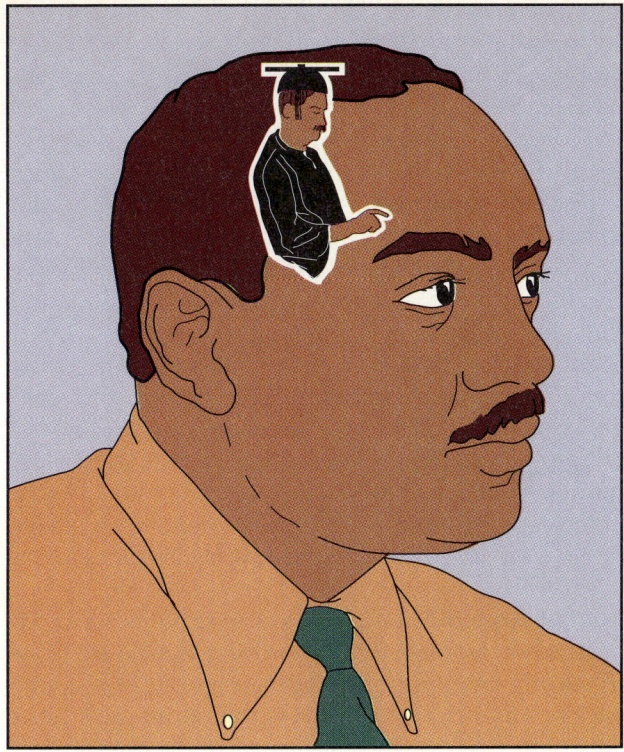

Meditation opens you up to the wisdom that is already within you.

shell, or rosary beads can also bring the mind to one thought.

Inclusive Meditation: The second type of meditation is called *inclusive meditation.* It is also referred to as *"access meditation," "insightful meditation,"* and *"mindfulness."* Inclusive meditation appears to be very similar to *free association,* in which the mind wanders aimlessly. In the practice of inclusive mediation, the mind is free to accept all thoughts from the conscious and unconscious mind. There is one condition, however. All thoughts that enter consciousness must do so objectively and without judgment or emotional attachment. This process is called *detached observation.* No emotional attachment can be connected with your thoughts. In effect, the mind becomes a wide movie screen with your thoughts projected as images, and you observe without judgment or analysis. Ideally, by separating yourself from your emotions, you allow the walls of your ego to dissolve temporarily, making you more open to ideas that help you resolve issues in your life. In this type of meditation, the eyes are usually open; however, if you prefer to close your eyes, this is fine.

The Relaxation Response   In his book *The Relaxation Response,* Dr. Herbert Benson describes how to meditate in four basic steps, resulting in a sense of calmness and tranquillity. The components are a quiet environment, a comfortable position, a mental device, and a passive attitude.

1. A quiet environment: A quiet environment can be anyplace where you can relax without distractions, where sounds of ringing phones and doorbells, blaring televisions or radios, even outside street noise are minimized. You might find the need to balance your environment with white (background) noise, perhaps some soft instrumental music.

2. A comfortable position: Eastern philosophy suggests that to relax the mind, you must first relax your body. So get into a comfortable position, with your back straight. The body should be relaxed, with no sense of muscular tension. If you feel that you might fall asleep, do this meditation sitting, not lying down.

3. A mental device: A mental device is any method used to replace all other thoughts. It is a focal point to direct all attention. A mental device can include the repetition of a mantra, diaphragmatic breathing, or a Zen koan (an unanswerable question such as "What is the sound of one hand clapping?"). You might wish to combine a repetitive mantra with diaphragmatic breathing as a mental device.

4. A passive attitude: A passive attitude is a receptive attitude, a frame of mind in which you are ready and willing to relax. A passive attitude has also been interpreted to include a state of physical calmness. If the body is extremely tense throughout the process, then the meditation session will not be as effective. In the words of Herbert Benson, "A passive attitude allows the meditative process to begin."

It has been said that in this high-tech age, we are seldom, if ever, in the presence of quality silence for any length of time. Because we continually get bombarded by messages and information, our minds end up getting choked. To keep your sanity, your mind has to unload these thoughts, or your entire well-

To illustrate the concept of the mind in concrete terms, clouds are often depicted as a metaphor to symbolize our thoughts, feelings, memories, and perceptions. Meditation acts like a strong wind that blows the clouds away and clears the mind of cluttered thoughts.

A mandala is circular in shape, symbolizing wholeness, and is often used throughout many cultures as an object of meditation.

being is at stake. The bottom line is that we all need regularly scheduled times of solitude to cleanse the cluttered mess of the mind.

Mental Imagery

Close your eyes for a moment, and listen to the gentle rolling waves of the ocean. See the clear, aqua-blue water of the waves as they break on the shore. Feel the white sand between your toes, the warm sun on your skin, and the soft wind as it caresses your face and continues on to sway the branches of a palm tree behind you. The salt air fills your senses, and as you exhale, you feel completely relaxed. Imagination is a powerful gift. When Einstein said that imagination was more powerful than knowledge, he meant that our wealth of knowledge is grounded in the depths of human imagination. As you know, your imagination can be used against you when problems become distorted, making mountains out of molehills. Yet your imagination can also serve as a tremendous defense against the effects of stress by creating relaxing images that are peaceful and restorative to your body.

In many ways, mental imagery is like making a motion picture. In this case, you take an active roles in being the *producer*, selecting the sets and scenery; the *director*, organizing the sensory cues; the *actor*, feeling and playing the part; and the *audience*, experiencing the effects of this production. Each role is equally important in making the image as powerful as possible. In simple terms, mental imagery is inten-

tional daydreaming. With practice, the use of this technique will enhance your skills in all these roles. You might find that this technique can be very enjoyable.

Mental imagery is a technique to access the powers of the conscious and unconscious mind to create a pictorial panorama that suggests calmness and tranquillity, much like taking a vacation. It is also now used as a healing tool to restore health to body organs caught in a state of dysfunction and disease (such as cancer) by imagining those organs in a healthy state. The skill of mental imagery involves the creation of images, scenes, or impressions by engaging your imagination of your body's physical senses of sight, sound, feel, smell, and even taste for a pleasurable mental sensation, such as going to the beach. In the case of a symbolic image, it could be the image of mending a broken bone or healing an ulcer.

Tranquil Natural Scenes   Natural settings are often selected to promote relaxation because nature is intrinsically calming to the human spirit. This is one reason why people vacation in the mountains or at the ocean side to escape the stress of the home or office environment. Images such as a tropical island beach, a mountain vista, or a path through an evergreen forest are commonly used. Once created, these natural scenes, full of vivid color, fresh air, natural sounds, and elements of nature, allow you to put your collective thoughts in true perspective. These natural scenes, like the real ones they imitate, have the ability to shrink perceptions and problems down to a manageable size, in proportion to the rest of the natural world. In essence, these tranquil im-

The best way to meditate is to find one place you can call your own where you can minimize distractions.

Sitting with your back straight and your legs comfortably crossed (known as the half-lotus position) helps decrease physical as well as mental distractions.

People often use a scene such as this, reminiscent of some vacation area, to promote relaxation.

ages turn distorted perceptions back into manageable thoughts. And although the visualization of these scenes will not make personal problems go away, they do appear to help shrink troubles to a tolerable size. More important, with the repeated practice of visualization, the heart rate and blood pressure begin to decrease, indicating a sense of calmness.

Of the all the natural settings that are used to promote relaxation, the most common are those that include water, such as ocean beaches, mountain lakes, and waterfalls and streams. However, any scene that you think is relaxing can have the same effect. The power of this type of imagery is to use not just the imagination of the visual sense, but those of the other body senses as well. To see the image, hear the sounds, smell the fragrances or freshness of the air, sense the air temperature, and feel the wind and the sun on your skin, all combine to create a powerful effect. By using all aspects of your imagination, you stop being a passive observer and become an *ac-*

Using the power of your imagination means looking beyond the normal view of conscious thought.

tive participant in your own image. Furthermore, by acknowledging all sensations, you experience firsthand the calming effects of this technique rather than being an outside observer.

Steps to Initiate Mental Imagery

1. **Assume a comfortable position:** Mental imagery, like diaphragmatic breathing, can be done almost anywhere—anyplace where you can close your eyes and tune out your current surroundings, allowing your imagination to create an image of peace and tranquillity. You can do this sitting or lying down.

2. **Concentration and attitude:** As with other relaxation techniques, mental imagery requires thorough concentration. Initial exposure to this technique may be short (5 minutes), allowing your powers of concentration to build. When using your sense of mental imagery, focus your attention on the vividness of colors, shapes, textures, sounds, noises, silence, smells, and the entire feel of the environment you have created. If your mind begins to wander away from this scene, try to steer your attention back to the details of the image. In terms of healing images such as cancerous tumors or broken bones, it is the experience of Drs. Bernie Siegel, Joan Borysenko, and Carl Simonton that *the belief* and *intention* in the power of the image are as important as the image itself.

3. **Visual themes:** Your choice of mental images is unlimited. You can begin by deciding what the purpose of your visualization is. Is it a momentary escape to clear your thoughts, or is the vision a healing image to restore and rejuvenate your body? Once you have decided, tailor your image to suit your needs, then close your eyes and go with it.

Mental imagery can be done anywhere at any time. It's very portable. Although it is best to learn

Using your imagination to create (or remember) a scene like this can help calm the mind and promote a sense of relaxation throughout the body.

mental imagery in a quiet environment, once you are proficient, you can use this technique at your work-site, on your break, or during your lunch hour. You can use it minutes before a professional presentation, waiting in line at the post office, sitting in the dentist's chair, attending a boring staff meeting, or in any situation in which you can briefly close your eyes to escape momentarily and regain some composure.

• EXERCISE 1 •
Breathing Clouds

This technique can be traced back to the origins of Eastern culture. It was introduced as a cleansing process for the mind and body in both yoga and Zen meditation. To begin, close your eyes, and focus all your attention on your breathing. Visualize the air that you take into your lungs as being clear, pure, energized air—air with the power to cleanse and heal your body. As you breathe in this clear, pure air, visualize and feel the air enter your nose (or mouth), travel up through the sinus cavity to the top of your head, and then continue down your spine and circulate throughout your lower stomach area. Now, as you exhale, visualize that the air leaving your body is dark air—dark, cloudy smoke that symbolizes all the stressors, frustrations, and toxins roaming throughout your mind and body. With each breath, allow the clean, pure air to enter and circulate and rejuvenate your body, and let the exhaled dark, dirty air help to rid your body of its stress and tension. Repeat this breathing cycle for 5–10 minutes. As you repeat this cycle of breathing clouds over and over again, notice the release of stress and tension. You might also notice the color of the exhaled air changing from black to gray, perhaps even to an off-white—a symbolic vision of complete relaxation.

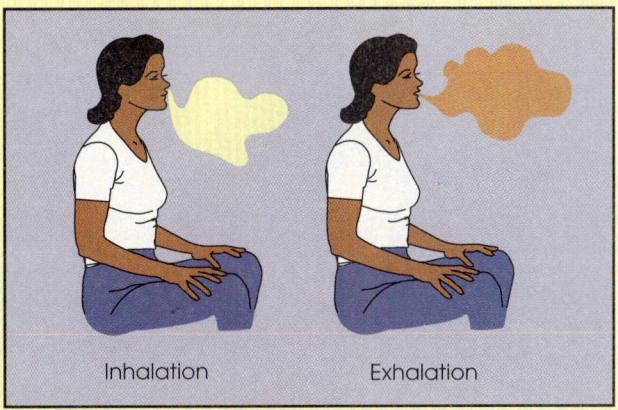

Inhalation　　　　Exhalation

Breathing clouds.

• EXERCISE 2 •
Relaxing Your Muscles

Muscle Group	100% Contraction	Release!	50% Contraction	Release!	5% Contraction	Release!
1. Face:	5 sec	45 sec	5 sec	45 sec	5 sec	45 sec
2. Jaws:	5 sec	45 sec	5 sec	45 sec	5 sec	45 sec
3. Neck:	5 sec	45 sec	5 sec	45 sec	5 sec	45 sec
4. Shoulders:	5 sec	45 sec	5 sec	45 sec	5 sec	45 sec
5. Upper chest:	5 sec	45 sec	5 sec	45 sec	5 sec	45 sec
6. Hands and forearms:	5 sec	45 sec	5 sec	45 sec	5 sec	45 sec
7. Abdominals:	5 sec	45 sec	5 sec	45 sec	5 sec	45 sec
8. Lower back:	5 sec	45 sec	5 sec	45 sec	5 sec	45 sec
9. Buttocks:	5 sec	45 sec	5 sec	45 sec	5 sec	45 sec
10. Thighs:	5 sec	45 sec	5 sec	45 sec	5 sec	45 sec
11. Calves:	5 sec	45 sec	5 sec	45 sec	5 sec	45 sec
12. Feet:	5 sec	45 sec	5 sec	45 sec	5 sec	45 sec

Facial stretch.

• EXERCISE 3 •
Autogenic Training

The following is a outline of the progression of instructions that you can repeat to yourself to practice this technique.

- Take a slow, deep breath, and feel the sense of relaxation throughout your body as you exhale. Repeat this again, making each breath even slower and deeper than the last.

Phase 1: Heaviness

- "My arms and hands feel heavy."
- "My legs and feet feel heavy."
- "My arms and legs feel heavy."

Phase 2: Warmth

- "My arms and hands feel warm."
- "My legs and feet feel warm."
- "My arms and legs feel warm."

Phase 3: Heart

- "My heart is calm and relaxed."
- "My heartbeat is slow and relaxed."

Phase 4: Breathing

- "My breathing is slow and relaxed."
- "My breathing is calm and comfortable."
- "My entire body is calm and relaxed."

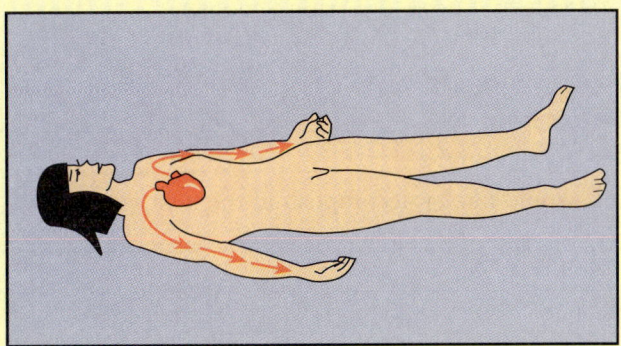

• EXERCISE 4 •
Your Target Heart Rate and Exercise Routine

To make sure that you are exercising at the right intensity for cardiovascular endurance, you should exercise in a target zone between 65% and 80% of your maximal capacity. Most people exercise at 75%; however, if you feel that you are out of condition you might wish to start at a lower intensity. To calculate your target heart rate, use the formula below. Then when you begin your exercise program, periodically check your heart rate to see whether you are hitting your target. If you find that you are above your target heart rate, you are working too hard and should slow down a bit.

Maximal heart rate = 220 (A constant value used by everyone)

       − _____ (Fill in your age here.)

       = _____ (Predicted maximal heart rate)

       − _____ (Subtract your resting heart rate here. You can determine your resting heart rate by taking your pulse for 60 seconds.)

       × .75 (Multiply 75% intensity of work load.)

       = _____ (Heart rate reserve)

       + _____ (Add back your resting heart rate.)

    * = _____ (Your target heart rate. *You can divide this number by 6 for a 10-second count to make it easier when monitoring your heart rate during exercise.)

       _____ (Divide by 6 for a 10-second count.)

What is your preferred type of exercise? _____

What time of day is best for you to exercise? _____

What three days are best for you to exercise? _____

What health and fitness goals would like to accomplish in the next year? _____

_____

_____

• EXERCISE 5 •
Floating Log Meditation

The floating log meditation is an exercise in which you close your eyes and imagine yourself sitting on a large rock by a river. As you look up the river, you see a log jam. Suddenly, you notice that the jam has begun to slowly break up. One by one, each log is set free and swiftly moves through the passive currents traveling downstream. As you see each log, place a thought on it, and then watch it slowly move out of sight. Take a slow deep breath, and observe the next log approach. Let this log carry another thought out of sight. Continue to free all the logs from the log jam until your mind seems completely free of thoughts.

- Try this while sitting comfortably in a chair or on the floor or lying down, keeping your spine aligned from your head to your hips.
- Observe your breathing, making each breath comfortably deep and relaxed.
- Use the log image as a repetitive visual mantra to help clear the mind of all thoughts.
- Initially, try this technique for about 5 minutes. Continue to add more time as your comfort level increases.

• EXERCISE 6 •

Hot Air Balloon Meditation

Close your eyes, and place yourself in the basket of a hot air balloon. The balloon is anchored firmly to the ground by several sandbags. Picture each sandbag as some problem that weighs you down and that you wish to let go of.

One by one, release each sandbag. Slowly, you begin to feel yourself getting lighter and lighter. Soon the balloon begins to lift off the ground. As you slowly rise up into the sky, feel yourself become lighter and lighter.

Sometimes using an image such as this can help clear the mind when meditating.

• EXERCISE 7 •
Creating Mental Images to Relax

When people think of peaceful scenes, they usually think of a natural setting. The best scenes seem to be far from the hustle and bustle of our everyday world, providing a retreat to nurture the soul. Now it's time for you to use your imagination and create some mental images of scenes that you feel are examples of peaceful retreats. Describe five mental images or peaceful, relaxing scenes in full detail that you would like to escape to momentarily. Remember to use all your senses, to place yourself at each scene. Be as elaborate as you can with the description so that it will remain vivid in your memory.

1.

2.

3.

4.

5.

5

A Healthier Lifestyle

The Big Picture • Purpose in Life
Letting Go of Stress: How to Maintain a Healthy Lifestyle

> *The winds of grace are blowing perpetually, we only need raise our sails.*
>
> —Sri Ramakrishna

The Big Picture

Today, people's attitudes, so strongly influenced by rushed lifestyles and the desire for immediate gratification, reflect a need to eradicate stress rather than manage, reduce, or control one's perceptions of it. As a result, stress never really goes away. It just reappears with a new face. Unfortunately, there are no magic bullets or quick fixes to deal with the tensions of everyday life. The tools to dismantle the "ticking clock" of perceived stress are best described as intangible, yet invaluable *inner resources*. These include, but are not limited to, patience, confidence, intuition, creativity, a sense of humor, courage, optimism, compassion, faith, and self-reliance.

To deal with stress effectively, we must truly learn to cultivate our inner resources. In an effort to understand stress, experts have looked at the physical, psychological, social, environmental, and spiritual aspects, and they have come to the conclusion that work must begin *within* each individual to make the transition from *stress-induced* behaviors toward a *stress-reduced* lifestyle. It is commonly agreed that as North America enters the twenty-first century, a greater need will develop for us to accept a bigger share of the responsibility for our own health and well-being. By knowing ourselves, our values, and our purpose in life, we can begin to gain a better perspective on ourselves, find a sense of balance in our day-to-day activities, and see how we fit into the bigger picture of life.

Focusing on yourself and nurturing personal growth in this day and age is not easy. Distractions in the form of television, phone calls, radios, and even extended work hours can block the process of nurturing the health of your human spirit. Uncentered and unbalanced, we become targets for everyday stressors. Making the time to nurture our own needs is not a selfish act. On the contrary, it is quite necessary. Like a portable phone that needs to be placed back in the cradle to recharge the battery, we to need to take time for ourselves so that we can recharge. The way to turn inward is often called the *centering process,* in which you allocate some quiet time to sit each day, collecting and reflecting on your thoughts and feelings. The fundamental purpose of every known coping and relaxation technique is to create the opportunity for the centering process. Once you become aware of the potential of your inner resources, you can use these during seemingly troubled times. Like the deep roots of a tree, they help to ground you and keep you from being "knocked over" by the winds of change. Psychologist Abraham Maslow called these inner resources traits of "self-actualization," in which a person learns to consciously move beyond the mundane and chaotic parts of life to appreciate life's real beauty and appreciate the bigger picture. The premise of a healthy life is to strike a balance between the time dedicated to work and time spent on ourselves. In the age of "Do more with less," this might be a challenge, but it is not impossible.

Purpose in Life

Medical experts were baffled when they discovered that first-time heart attack patients often showed few,

Making time for yourself to become centered and grounded is not a selfish act; it is essential for your own wellbeing.

following are some ideas to incorporate into your daily lifestyle to help meet less resistance.

1. Learn to **respond** rather than react to situations that you find upsetting or a violation of your rights as an individual.
2. Learn to **refine your expectations** and build a healthy tolerance toward situations that often disturb your inner balance.
3. Randomly **give yourself positive feedback** by way of daily affirmations to validate your own self-esteem and worthiness. Self-esteem, like a house plant, needs regular attention. This practice might seem awkward at first, but give it a try.
4. Make it a habit to **get out and exercise** to burn off any residual stress hormones that may be circulating in your body from a stressful day at the office. When your motivation is low, remember that walking is a great form of exercise.
5. **Balance your scale of emotions** with some comic relief by incorporating some humor and mirth into your daily routine.
6. **Nurture your connectedness** with the people in your circle of friends and family. If you feel that your personal network is lacking in support, then take the time to meet new people with similar interests and build new relationships.

if any, of the known risk factors associated with heart disease. The most common characteristic is now reported to be job dissatisfaction. Many experts equate this with a lack of meaning in one's life. This observance correlates highly with the fact that more heart attacks occur on Monday morning between 8:00 and 10:00 A.M. than at any other time during the week. Though much more difficult to measure than cholesterol and blood pressure, a meaningful purpose in life is now thought to be a critical factor in maintaining one's health. This can be seen most readily with the sudden death of bereaved spouses, retirees, and people who have their career set back by downsizing. Establishing (or reestablishing) and evaluating your purpose in life also involves time to center and ground yourself. These coping and relaxation techniques are vehicles to assist you in this process.

Letting Go of Stress: How to Maintain a Healthy Lifestyle

It is fair to say that the greatest percentage of daily stressors are based on the issue of control. In many cases, we expend much time and energy trying to influence and manipulate people or things over which we have no control. This is what letting go of stress is all about: focusing on the Self, exerting control over ourselves (employing willpower), rather than focusing on events and people within our environment over which we have no control. It might take some effort, but the task of letting go of stress is not impossible; eventually it is quite liberating.

The creation of a stress management program is a very personal undertaking because no two people are alike. Yet despite our differences, there are several suggestions that we can follow in making our life journey less troublesome and more enjoyable. The

"The meaning of life, and make it snappy -- we're double parked."

Source: Stratton.

The answers to the meaning of your life come from a continual soul-searching process, not an outside source.

7. **Diversify your interests and activities** so that your whole identity is not wrapped up into your career or paycheck. This will not only make a bad day at the office more tolerable, it can actually improve your attitude about work as well.

8. **Learn to recognize and become comfortable with all your emotions,** spanning the spectrum from anger to love, and learn to express these emotions creatively and productively.

Achieving a goal or life purpose is one of many ways to nurture the health of the human spirit.

Success

- To laugh often and love much
- To win the respect of intelligent persons and the affection of children
- To earn the approval of honest critics and endure the betrayal of false friends
- To appreciate beauty
- To find the best in others
- To give of oneself without the slightest thought of return
- To have accomplished a task, whether by a healthy child, a rescued soul, a garden patch, or a redeemed social connection
- To have played and laughed with enthusiasm and sung with exultation
- To know that even one life has breathed easier because you have lived.

—Anonymous

9. **Exercise your sense of creativity,** and use this talent as well as other inner resources to relieve stress at the worksite.

10. **Learn to resolve issues and concerns with others** *when they arise,* through peaceful and diplomatic confrontation rather than avoidance.

11. **Take short breaks in the course of each working day to relax** and give your body a chance to return to a normal resting state.

12. Make it a habit every day to **dedicate personal time for you** and you alone without feeling guilty. Take a few moments at the start or end of each day to sit quietly and meditate or reflect on who you are and where you are going in your life. Start with as little as 5 minutes, and build up from there.

• EXERCISE 1 •
A Look Within

The following are some questions that you might want to think about to strengthen your inner resources and the health of the human spirit. Spend a few minutes pondering these questions, and then write down your thoughts here.

The following attributes or inner resources are considered important tools to deal effectively with stress. Rate your sense of potential with these qualities (1 = poor, 10 = excellent).

Attribute	Poor									Excellent
Patience	1	2	3	4	5	6	7	8	9	10
Confidence	1	2	3	4	5	6	7	8	9	10
Intuition	1	2	3	4	5	6	7	8	9	10
Creativity	1	2	3	4	5	6	7	8	9	10
Sense of humor	1	2	3	4	5	6	7	8	9	10
Courage	1	2	3	4	5	6	7	8	9	10
Optimism	1	2	3	4	5	6	7	8	9	10
Compassion	1	2	3	4	5	6	7	8	9	10
Faith	1	2	3	4	5	6	7	8	9	10
Self-reliance	1	2	3	4	5	6	7	8	9	10

1. How well do I really know myself? How have my beliefs, attitudes, and opinions changed from just five years ago?

2. What aspects in life do I really value? What are the things that are most important in my life? Do I spend time living my values? Are some values in conflict with each other?

3. Where am I headed with my life? How would I define my life purpose at this time? Am I making progress toward it or do I seem to be in a period of stagnation?

4. What have I learned from my past experiences and how can I use these lessons to guide my life journey?

References and Resources

You might find that many topics in this workbook merit more attention. The following books can provide more information on the topics of mental, physical, emotional, and spiritual well-being.

Archterberg, Jean, *Imagery and Healing. Shamanism and Modern Medicine.* Boston: Shambhala Publications, 1985.

Beattie, Melodie, *Codependent No More.* New York: Hazelton/Harper Press, 1987.

Beattie, Melodie, *Beyond Codependence.* New York: Hazelton/Harper Press, 1989.

Benson, Herbert, *The Relaxation Response.* New York: Morrow Press, 1975.

Borysenko, Joan, *Minding the Body, Mending the Mind.* New York: Bantam Books, 1984.

Borysenko, Joan, *Fire in the Soul, A New Psychology of Spiritual Optimism.* New York: Warner Books, 1993.

Buscaglia, Leo, *Love.* New York: Fawcett Crest, 1972.

Buscaglia, Leo, *Living, Loving and Learning.* New York: Fawcett Books, 1982.

Casey, Karin, and Martha Vanceburg, *The Promise of a New Day.* New York: Harper & Row, 1983.

Chopra, Deepak, *Quantum Healing.* New York: Bantam Books, 1989.

Cooper, Kenneth, *The Aerobics Program for Total Well-being.* New York: Bantam Books, 1983.

Covey, Steven, *The Seven Habits of Highly Effective People.* New York: Fireside/Simon and Schuster, 1989.

Dossey, Larry, *Recovering the Soul.* New York: Bantam Books, 1989.

Dossey, Larry, *Meaning and Medicine.* New York: Bantam Books, 1991.

Dossey, Larry, *Healing Words, The Power of Prayer and the Practice of Medicine.* San Francisco: HarperCollins, 1993.

Dyer, Wayne, *Your Erroneous Zones.* New York: Avon Books, 1976.

Fanning, Patrick, *Visualization for Change.* Oakland, CA: New Harbinger Publications, 1988.

Foster, Steven, *The Book of the Vision Quest, by Steven* with Meredith Little, New York: Prentice Hall Press, 1988.

Frankl, Viktor, *Man's Search for Meaning.* New York: Pocket Books, 1984.

Gawain, Shakti, *Creative Visualization.* San Rafael, CA: New World Library, 1978.

Jacobson, Edmund, *You Must Relax.* New York: McGraw-Hill, 1978.

Jampolski, Gerald, *Love Is Letting Go of Fear.* Berkeley, CA: Celestial Arts, 1979.

Jung, Carl, *Man and His Symbols.* New York: Anchor Press, 1964.

Klein, Allen, *The Healing Power of Humor.* Los Angeles: J.P. Tarcher, 1989.

Kübler-Ross, Elisabeth, *On Life After Death.* Berkeley, CA: Celestial Arts, 1991.

Lerner, Harriet, *The Dance of Anger.* New York: Harper & Row, 1985.

Lindbergh, Anne Morrow, *Gift from the Sea.* New York: Vintage Books, 1978.

Moyers, Bill, *Healing and the Mind.* New York: Anchor Press, 1993.

Peck, M. Scott, *The Road Less Traveled.* New York: Touchstone Press, 1978.

Peter, Lawrence, and Bill Dana, *The Laughter Prescription.* New York: Ballantine Press, 1982.

Roman, Sanaya, *Spiritual Growth, Being Your Higher Self.* Tiburon, CA: HJ Kramer Inc., 1989.

Seaward, Brian Luke, *Managing Stress, Principles and Strategies for Health and Wellbeing.* Boston: Jones and Bartlett Publishers, 1994.

Selye, Hans, *Stress without Distress.* New York: Signet Books, 1974.

Siegel, Bernie, *Love, Medicine & Miracles.* New York: Perennial Press, 1987.

Siegel, Bernie, *Peace, Love, & Healing.* New York: Perennial Press, 1990.

Simonton, O. Carl, Stephanie Simonton, and James Creighton, *Getting Well Again.* New York: Bantam Books, 1978.

von Oech, Roger, *A Whack on the Side of the Head.* New York: Warner Books, 1983.

von Oech, Roger, *A Kick in the Seat of the Pants.* New York: Perennial Library, 1986.

Weisinger, Harold, *The Anger Workout Book.* Harlington, TX: Quill Books, 1985.

Index

stressors
  acute, 2
  chronic, 2
  identifying, 5
stress-prone personality traits, 17
stress-resistant personality
    traits, 17
stress response, 2–3
sugar, 48
summarizing, in conversation, 28
support networks, 32, 39
suppression, 7
surrender, as conflict management
    style, 31

tactile motion, repetitive, 50
target heart rate, exercise and, 58
technology, stress and, 34
temporomandibular joint dysfunction
    (TMJ), 10
tension headaches, 10
tension release, 43, 44
Three C's method, 25
Three P's method, 25

time allocation, 25
time juggling, 24–25
time management, 24–28, 35–37
  roadblocks to, 24–25
  techniques, 25–27
TMJ, 10
toxic thoughts, 18–19
tranquil natural scenes, mental
    imagery of, 52–53
Type A personality, 17, 24

ulcers, 11
underhanders, 7
uniqueness, self-esteem and, 8
United Nations, 3

victimization, 18
visual concentration, 50
visualization, 52–54
  diaphragmatic breathing and, 43
vitamin deficiencies, 48, 49
vocabulary, communication skills and,
    28, 29
von Oech, Roger, 21

warm-up period, for exercise workout,
    47–48
warrior phase, of creative process, 22
white blood cells, 10, 12
withdrawal, as conflict management
    style, 31
word prejudice, 28
workaholism, time management
    and, 24
workday, length of, 4
workouts. See also exercise
  phases of, 47–48
workplace stress, 1, 3–4
  causes of, 4
  costs of, 3
  environmental causes of, 4
  individual causes of, 4
  organizational causes of, 4
  profile, 5
  self-esteem and, 8–9